Disclaimer

The intention of this book is not to replace me

consulting a physician. If you are sick or not medicall physical training, you should see a physician before beginning any fitness training. **If you are taking prescription medication, you should never change your diet without first consulting your physician as any dietary change will affect the action of that prescription drug.**

As with any new fitness activity, regardless of your fitness background, you must start out slowly. Too much, too soon is one of the most common reasons for the failure of a new routine. It is also likely to result in injury. Even well-conditioned athletes will experience discomfort or injuries while undergoing new types of training if they push themselves too hard. Remember, the whole aim of fitness training is to enhance life, not shorten it.

Although this book is about fitness, nutrition and mental conditioning, the author and publisher disclaim responsibility for any adverse effects arising from extreme exercise and dieting and the use of nutritional supplements without appropriate medical supervision.

Stomach Flattening

Training Manual

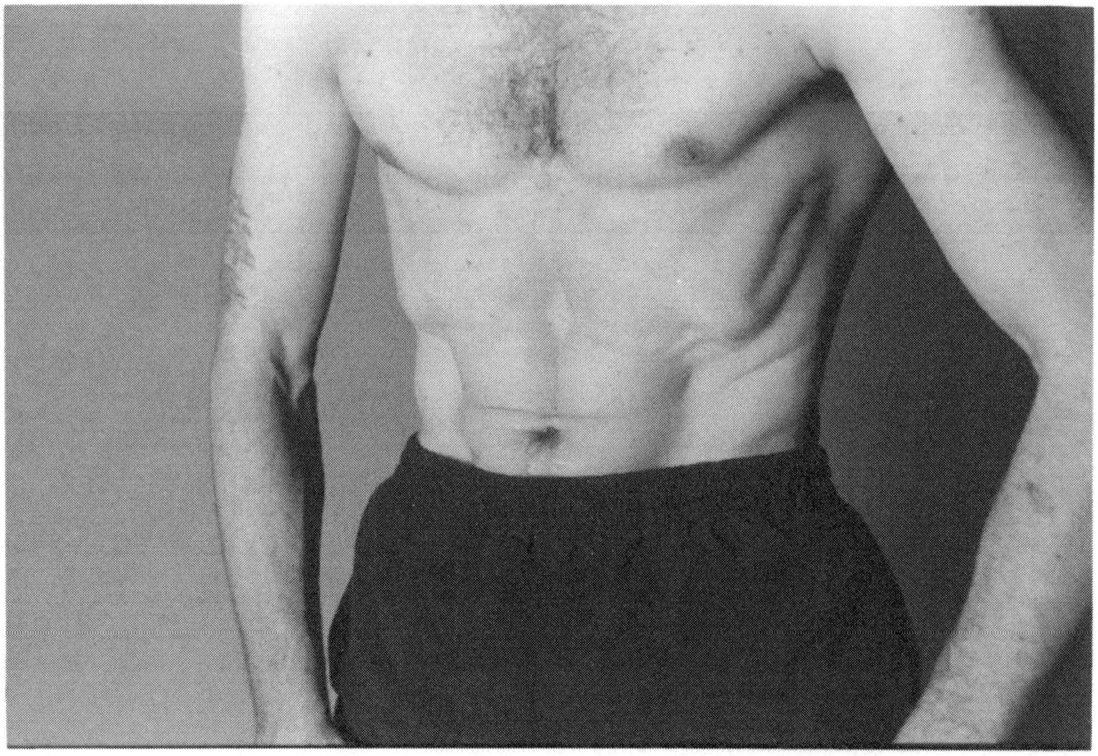

Published by Resilience Press

ISBN – 13: 978-0973182521
ISBN –10: 0973182521

Black and white photography by Perry Fiedler
Models: Doug Setter, Susan Hrynchuk, Laura Wiebe
Exercise diagrams from Physigraph Clipart (www.physigraphe.com)

Table of Contents

Introduction: The Flat Stomach Mind-Set

How does a stomach get so flat?

Is it simply a matter of genetics, what you have at birth is what you are stuck with for life? Does a trim midriff suddenly bloat itself during a weekend getaway? Does a beer belly miraculously vanish after an intense afternoon of yard work? Except in some rare cases, the answer to all of these questions is “No”.

The flat stomach or the not-so-flat stomach gets that way from years and years of habits. Genetics and accidents aside, our minds and bodies are the result of our daily actions. As a yoga master commented, “the body is built by the mind behind it”.[i]

This does not mean a life sentence of celery and carrot sticks coupled with marathon runs. Nor does it require that you follow every trendy diet that comes along; take magic pills; buy state-of-the art exercise equipment; or undergo surgery. (Note: Despite the rate of success of gastric bypass surgery, it is still a drastic measure with serious health consequences. One of the reasons that a gastric bypass — also known as stomach stapling — is often successful is because following the operation the patient can eat only very small meals. This means the individual has no choice but to change their behavior, otherwise they will become seriously ill. They must also be on constant watch for complications for the rest of their lives. In this way, the patient has no choice but to be aware of their health. With such serious consequences, I would not recommend gastric bypass for weight loss.)

The truth is that developing and maintaining a flat stomach is far less complicated than most people believe. Although it requires a certain amount of consistency and discipline, achieving a flat stomach, like so many other things in life, is simply a matter of establishing small, regular routines that can be incorporated into your everyday activities. Whether you are striving for a flat stomach, a university degree or a higher income, the bottom line is that your success will mainly depend on the habits you keep. In this book, I want to get you doing the little things that will give you a strong, flat stomach in the shortest time possible.

Chapter 1: Why a Flat Stomach?

It is truly amazing just how much the whole body relies on the lower back and abdominal muscles for support. I found this out firsthand as a teenager after having my appendix removed. I remember how I felt in those first days after the surgery when almost every movement was agony and the only way I could walk was hunched over like I had osteoporosis. During that time, I forgot all about my struggling quest for a big chest and muscular arms to go with it. I just wanted to walk upright again. It was a simple yet powerful revelation: you are only as strong as your back, and your abdominal muscles support your back.

Strong abdominals can also protect against injury from hard physical labor, accidents or even contact sports. I have definitely relied on my strong abdominal and back muscles as a competitive kick-boxer and for activities such as tactical parachuting in my career with the military. Even from a cosmetic point of view, a person definitely looks better if the muscles around their core are strong and they are not hobbling around as the result of an injury.

Internally, a strong abdominal wall minimizes the likelihood of hernias as well as some digestive and back problems. It also goes a long way to being healthier and feeling better. The amount of weight that you carry around your waist can determine future health problems. It is a scientific fact that being fatter around the middle (apple shaped) is worse than having excess fat around the hips and thighs (pear shaped). Too high of a

Waist-Hip-Ratio (WHR) is unhealthy. If you have a wider waist than hips, then you have a higher than normal risk for high blood pressure, heart disease, stroke, diabetes and even some forms of cancer.[ii]

You can test your WHR by dividing the narrowest circumference of your waist with the widest part of your hips. For instance, a 32 inch waist divided by 36 inch hips equals .8. Guys are allowed a maximum ratio of 1.0 and the ladies are allowed up to .8.

In addition to all the other reasons for keeping your abdominals strong, a flat belly just plain looks good. While starving societies admire large stomachs, the western world is unusually hard on overweight people. Most cartoon villains are overweight. Even children have described silhouette pictures of overweight people as "cheaters, lazy or mean".[iii] A flat gut might not make you rich, famous and popular with the opposite sex. But, a strong abdominal wall of muscle does go a long way to being healthier and feeling better.

Chapter 2: Basic Abdominal Anatomy

Without getting too technical, in this chapter we will cover some of the basic abdominal and back muscle groups.

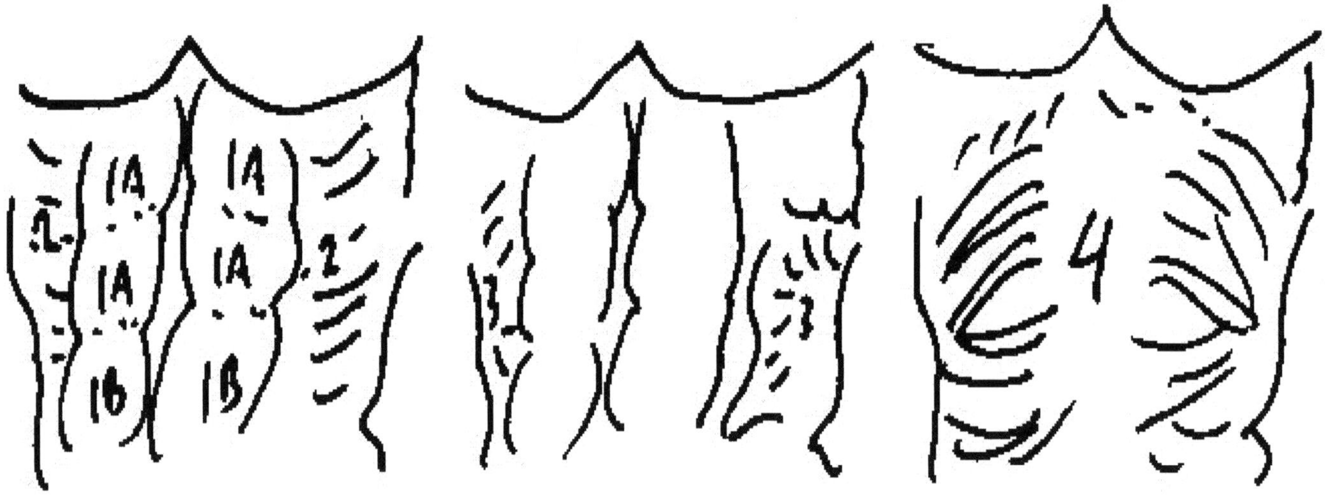

Rectus abdominus. (1A upper, 1B lower). These are often seen as two rows of washboard-like muscles. The three most noticeable muscle packets are often referred to as a "six-pack". These muscles flex the body forward and are essential for jumping, running and lifting.

The external obliques (2) are attached from the lower eight ribs to the rectus abdominus. These muscles flex the body sideways and twist the trunk, which is useful for golf, hockey and tennis.

The internal obliques (3) attach from the hip to lumbar (lower back) tissue, underneath the external obliques. These muscles also aid in side flexion and twisting the trunk, which is useful for swimming, skating and other activities that involve lower body twisting.

The transverse abdominus (4) runs horizontally across the abdominal wall along the midsection. This is worth noting as the tightening of these muscles forces your breath out. These muscles are used in activities that demand short bursts of effort as is required by singers, boxers and martial artists. Learning to use these traverse muscles properly can improve your abdominal workouts within as little as seven days. This is where breathing becomes so important.

Chapter 3: Posture and Breathing

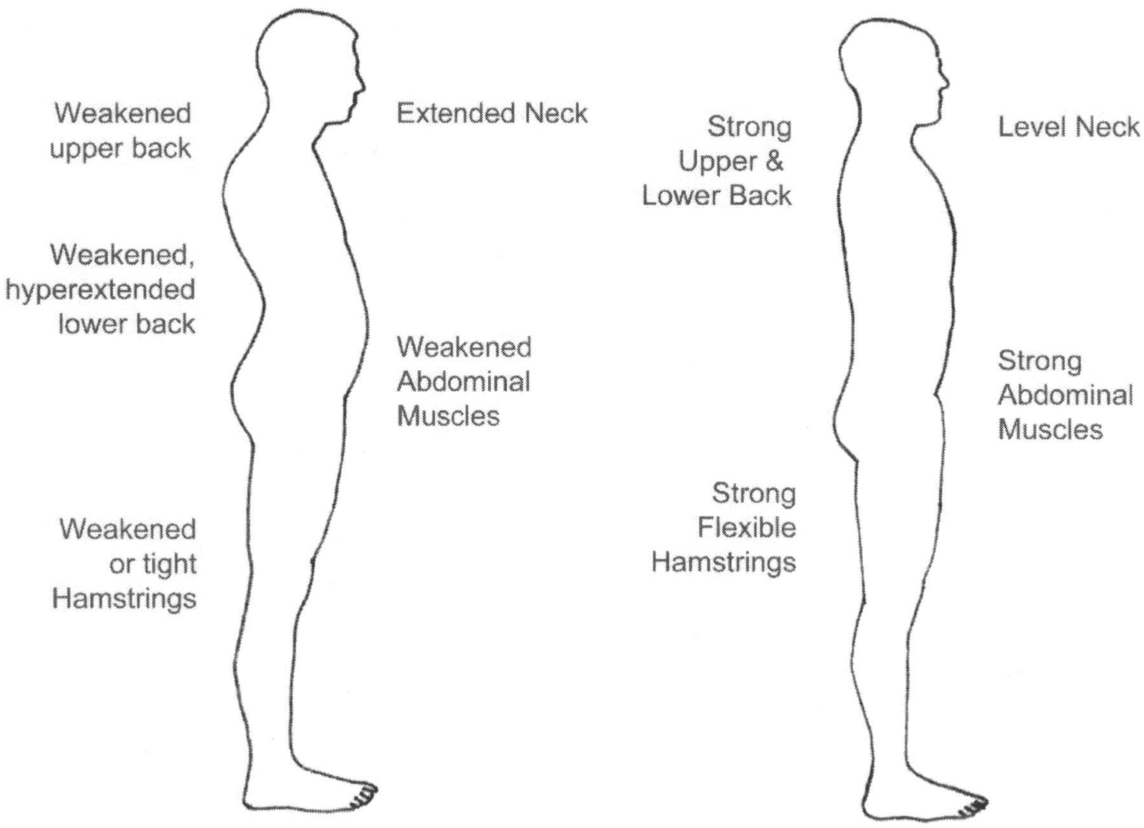

POSTURE AND HEALTH

Strong stomach muscles and flexible hamstrings are essential to good back health. If you think of the human spine as a tent pole and the body's muscles as the guy lines that stretch out and keep it standing upright, then you can understand how the muscles around the trunk support the whole body. Strong back and stomach muscles result in a sturdy structure. Therefore, as a human structure you are only as strong as your back and in turn, your back is only as strong as the stomach muscles that support it.

You only have to walk down any busy street to notice just how many people have improper posture. Office workers for example, are noticeable for their rounded shoulders and the exaggerated curve of their lower back. This is often the result of long hours of chair sitting. As we sit for extended periods of time, the upper body slouches, the head leans forward, intestines hang below the rib cage and the hamstrings tighten. To top it off, after eight hours of this kind of abuse, the average desk jockey heads home behind a steering wheel or on a cramped bus. Once home, they flop in front of the television and mindlessly stare at the T.V. screen until bedtime. With no tightening or adjustment of the muscle "guy-lines," over time the human structure inevitably weakens.

Posture is much more than cosmetics or dinner table etiquette. Posture is the strong alignment of the body. It allows for better digestion, circulation and ease of movement. This is why posture is part of many healthy living programs such as the martial arts and yoga. Posture also reflects how you present yourself to the world and how you project your confidence or lack thereof.

A strong posture allows the human spine to curve naturally. If you were to hang a plumb bob alongside your body, it would run along the ear, the shoulder joint, the hip joint, the middle of the knee and the anklebone. To check your own posture, a crude reference point is to stand with your heels, back and head against a wall. With these points in contact with the wall, there should be approximately a hand thickness of space between the small of your back and the wall.

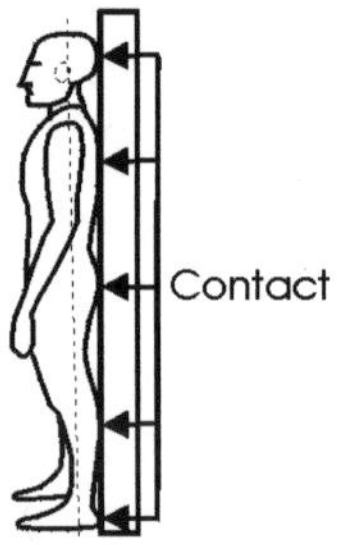

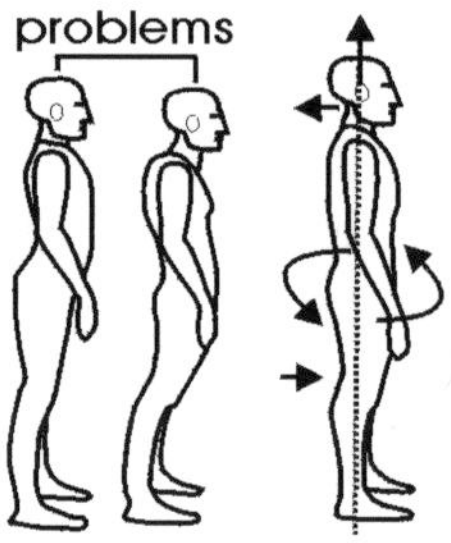

As mentioned previously, most people have the forward head and slouched upper body, otherwise known as Kordosis. Other weakened or misaligned back conditions are the sway back (a kind of a bow-shaped posture), the “duck back”, (as seen in many military types with a flat back and protruding butt) and the flat back (with this condition, there is a straight line from the neck down to the legs caused from over-tight hamstrings and back muscles). This last condition is notable because at first glance the person appears to have no butt and it would seem that only imagination or a good set of suspenders is holding up their pants.

While some people who are trying to correct their posture place little signs that say “posture” around their homes and workplaces, maintaining good posture is far easier when the back and stomach muscles are strong and flexible.

BREATHING FOR GREATER ENERGY

Next to a weak posture, a person's breathing pattern is the next dead give away to their fitness level. Fit people tend to breathe slower and easier. Unfit people tend to gasp and pant. When you watch animals or children playing, they will run themselves to exhaustion, stop, catch their breath and then run around some more. The average adult acts terrified of taking in a healthy lungful of air. It is as if they have forgotten how to breathe. This really is a tragedy since when you run out of breath you run out of performance, period. You can pick out most of the unfit people during an exercise class. They are the ones who are choking and gasping in the back of the room. People with low stamina usually hold their breath or pant when they exercise. Fitter people tend to take longer, calmer breaths. Watch professional athletes in action and you will often see them breathing calmly and deeply.

Controlling my breathing helped me win a welterweight kick-boxing championship against a younger, fitter opponent. By the fourth round, he was out of breath — and out of gas — at which point his coach threw in the towel.

Proper breathing increases the absorption of oxygen into the blood. The co-ordination of breathing with exercise helps relax muscles and release tension, especially in the neck, shoulders and mid-back. Strong exhalation can draw strength from the deep support muscles. This is why weightlifters and martial artists often yell or shout as they exhale. This allows them to bring muscles into play that they do not normally use.

To make the most of your effort, during most abdominal exercises, breathe out while contracting your abdominals. This will give you deeper contractions and harder, more defined muscles. You will also be getting better results for your efforts than the red-faced beginner who grunts through a basic routine.

To understand what I'm talking about, try the following experiment: take a deep breath and then hold it while performing a crunch[iv] or sit up. Not much fun is it? Now try letting your breath out as you do a crunch or sit up. It might feel strange, but it should be easier. **Note: It is too much carbon dioxide rather than not enough oxygen that causes fatigue. This is why it is essential to breathe out stale air during exercise.**

Deep breathing is a long-lost ability for most people. With the exception of singers, public speakers, marksmen, martial artists and some athletes, most people gobble down bits of air mostly through their upper and middle lungs. This restricted breathing uses as little as one-tenth of one's own natural lung capacity![v]

Fortunately, proper breathing and exercise can improve most of these conditions within a few weeks. Most of these breathing exercises can be done at your desk, in your car or waiting at a bus stop and even with casual practice, the benefits are noticeable.

For those who would like a little more formal breath training, consider the following techniques that can be practiced just about anywhere. However, do not be fooled by the simplicity of these exercises; they are simple, but effective. Try them and reap the benefits.

BREATHING EXERCISES

1. Take a deep breath and then force all of the air out of your lungs. When you think that you cannot exhale any more, tighten your abdominals and force out a little more air (do this three times). Repeat this exercise three or four times throughout the day with a few hours break in between. At first it will feel like you are running out of air and you might start coughing and feel a bit dizzy. If performed correctly, you should feel this deep in the lower abdominals. Usually it takes about five to ten sessions to learn to do this properly and then it becomes a habit.

2. Next, repeat the first exercise, but exhale while pressing your lips against your teeth allowing only a small slit for the air to escape. This will force your transverse abdominal muscles to contract. Some yoga textbooks claim that this also helps remove toxins from the blood.[vi]

3. The next exercise, called the Complete Breath is a bit more advanced. First, inhale into your lower lungs (this will make your abdominal wall actually swell a bit). Next, expand your ribcage and lastly, raise your collarbone. By contracting the abdominals, THEN the ribcage and FINALLY the upper chest, you can achieve a wave-like motion. Although it may feel awkward at first, the Complete Breath can be learned within a week and has been used to treat serious breathing conditions such as asthma.[vii] In one variation, asthmatic children are taught this technique by having them lie on their back with a rubber duck on their stomach. They are then encouraged to perform the Complete Breath by making a wave with their abdominals. If you want to try this at home and are missing a rubber duck, a paperback book will do the trick. Eventually, you will find that you can do this exercise sitting up at your desk or in your car.

If you are still feeling that you cannot get the breathing right, we can solve your problem right here and now by reuniting you with your natural born ability to breathe deeply with one of two surefire methods. The first method is to have you sprint up a hill several times in succession. The second, and more immediate method, is to have you jump into cold water (a cold shower will fit the bill nicely). If you care to try either of these methods, I guarantee that your heart and lungs will immediately kick into high gear and you will have no trouble whatsoever, drawing in long, deep breaths. In fact, you probably will not be thinking of much else except your next lungful of air!

I myself have rediscovered this cold water treatment several times over the years. I first read about it in a book called *Zen Combat* (by Jay Gluck) and later in *Chinese Boxing: Masters and Methods* (by Robert W. Smith). It also comes highly recommended by naturopathic doctors and old time fitness pioneers like Paul C. Bragg and Jack Lalanne. Champion grappler Matt Furey also advocates cold showers.

Another take on the cold shower is the polar bear plunge. For several years, some friends and I would go Polar Bear swimming on New Year's Day, in Vancouver, Canada. It was always good for a laugh, not to mention the fact that it was a great way to clear a hangover and, I must add, contrary to popular belief, no one ever got sick from doing it. For me, there is nothing quite like bringing in the New Year with a plunge into cold water. Also, as masochistic as it might seem to some people, it is also a great way to kick-start the day and it reminds us in less than a couple of heartbeats about the importance of deep breathing.

By now, I'm sure that most of you have found several excuses not to try this little breathing experiment. "Wait-a-minute!" you're saying. "I can't believe this guy is telling me to go jump in freezing cold water". Well, here is where we can separate the doers from the talkers. So you can either start practicing those breathing exercises right now or, alternatively, go hop into some cold water. It's nice to have options, isn't it?

Polar Bear Swim, New Year's Day, Vancouver, B.C. Canada

Chapter 4: Abdominal Exercises

Drawing-in-the-abdomen

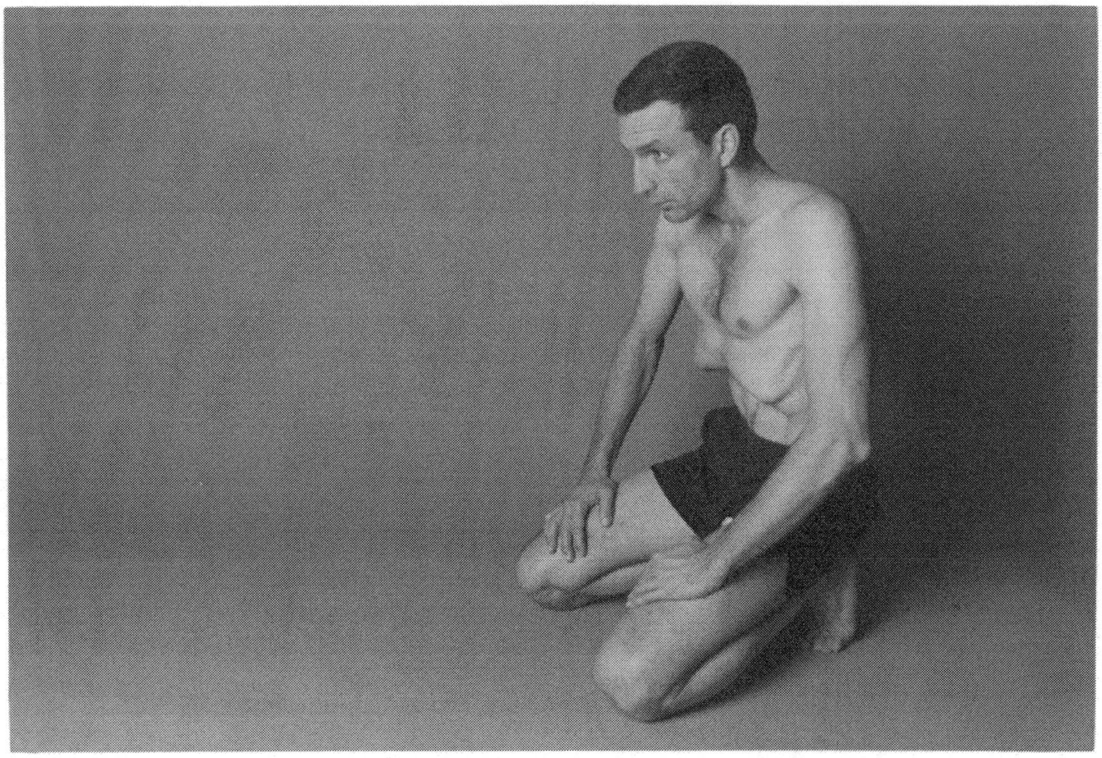

This is an instinctive exercise when on the beach. It also often happens subconsciously when a guy is wearing swim trunks in the presence of females. While it might look and feel a bit foolish, it is highly under-rated as a stomach toning exercise. For those of you who are familiar with yoga, it is basically the same exercise as the hatha yoga asana, Uddiyanna-bandha and it is goes like this:

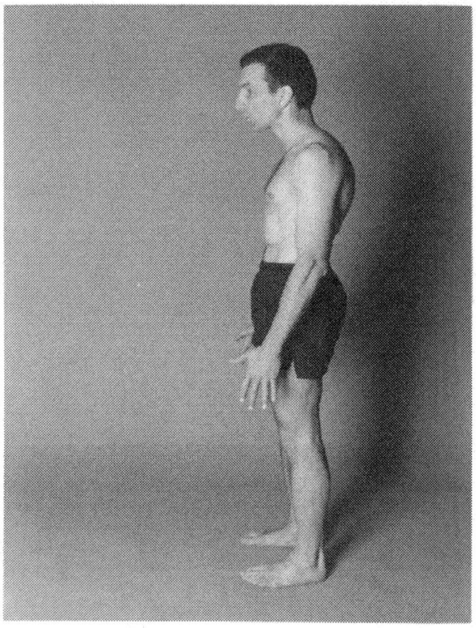 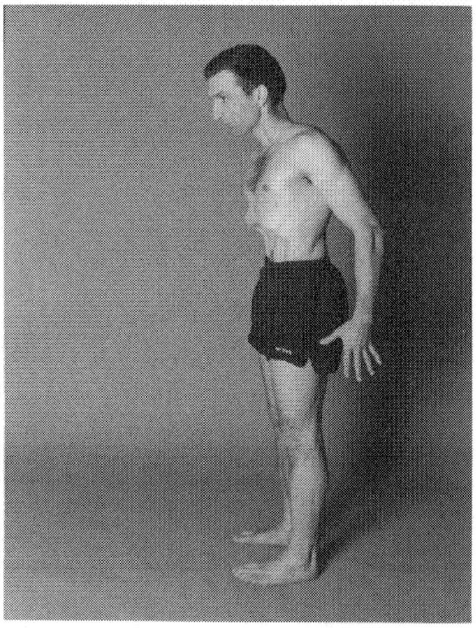

1. As with the first breathing exercise, while standing or sitting upright, take a deep breath and exhale fully.
2. While holding your breath, draw in your stomach (i.e. suck in your gut).
3. Now hold it for a few seconds (try a slow count of ten).
4. Relax and inhale.

You can start out standing, sitting or kneeling, then later progress to arching your back while pressing down on your thighs. A more advanced technique is to exhale while bending forward at the waist.

Be advised, you should only practice this exercise on an empty stomach. Start out two or three times per day and increase your repetitions gradually. As this movement tones the internal organs, it often causes another kind of movement. So, expect more regular trips to the washroom as your body might be doing a bit of house cleaning.

This is a great exercise for the abdominals and internal organs. Once you have mastered this technique, it will stay with you for life and you can practice it almost anywhere. In fact, you should be able to do it right where you are while reading this book. It really is that simple.

Variations

1. Exhale, hold your breath and then move the gut in and out several times.
    a. Beginners: 3-4 sets of 10 repetitions
    b. Intermediate: 3-4 sets of 25 repetitions
    c. Advanced: 2 sets of 50 repetitions

A Hung Gar kung fu sifu (instructor) I once took classes with used to perform this exercise at the beginning of each workout. Although he rarely did western abdominal exercises like crunches, he had a rock-solid gut. He could take punches and kicks to the midriff without flinching. After a few months of training with just the breathing exercises, punches and kicks, everyone in the class developed a solid midriff. Even the heavy beer drinkers in our class toned up their beer muscles and lost their personal “beer kegs”.

2. To exercise the sides of the waist, around the "handles", draw in the gut while pressing lightly with one hand on your thigh and tilting your body to that side.

Isometrics

Isometric exercise is exercise that works and develops the muscles without excessive movement. A good example of isometrics is the experiment that showed how a frog's legs, when tied together for short periods over a matter of days, would become stronger simply from the act of straining against the strings that held the legs together. Isometrics is the basis for the popular Charles Atlas muscle-building course. The following six-second exercises can be performed almost anywhere.

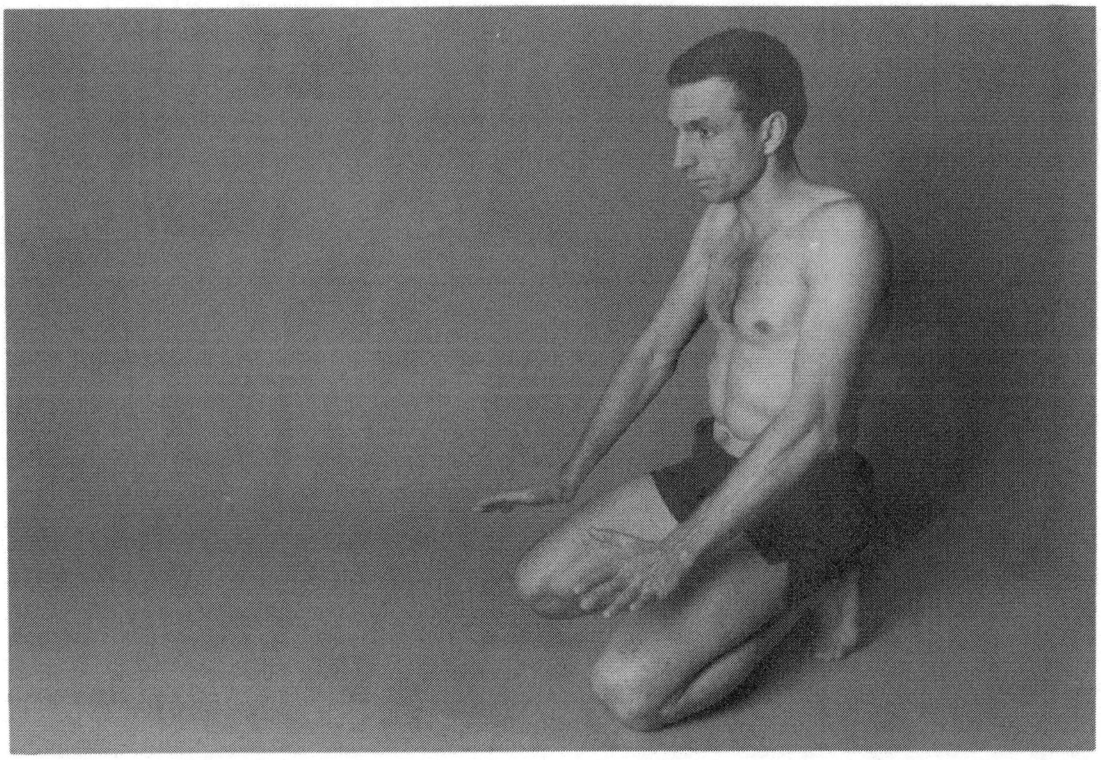

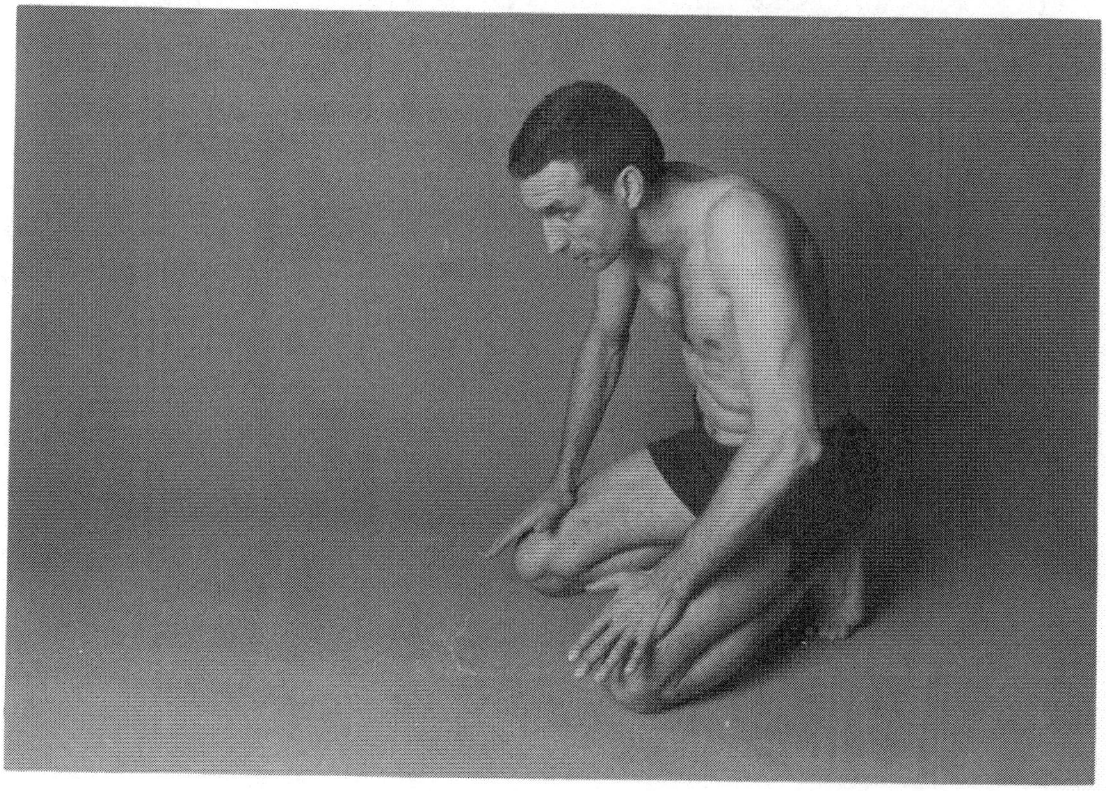

1. While standing, sitting or kneeling, take a deep breath and push down on your thighs. Exhale while you push down and try to bring your ribcage into your hips. After six seconds, release the pressure and take a few deep breaths. Repeat the exercise a couple more times.
2. Repeat the above while pushing down with one hand on an object (e.g. the window ledge) or a thigh. Relax after six seconds and repeat using the other hand.
3. While sitting, lean back until your stomach feels tight and then twist to one side. Hold for six seconds and then repeat twisting to the other side.

Isometric stomach vacuum

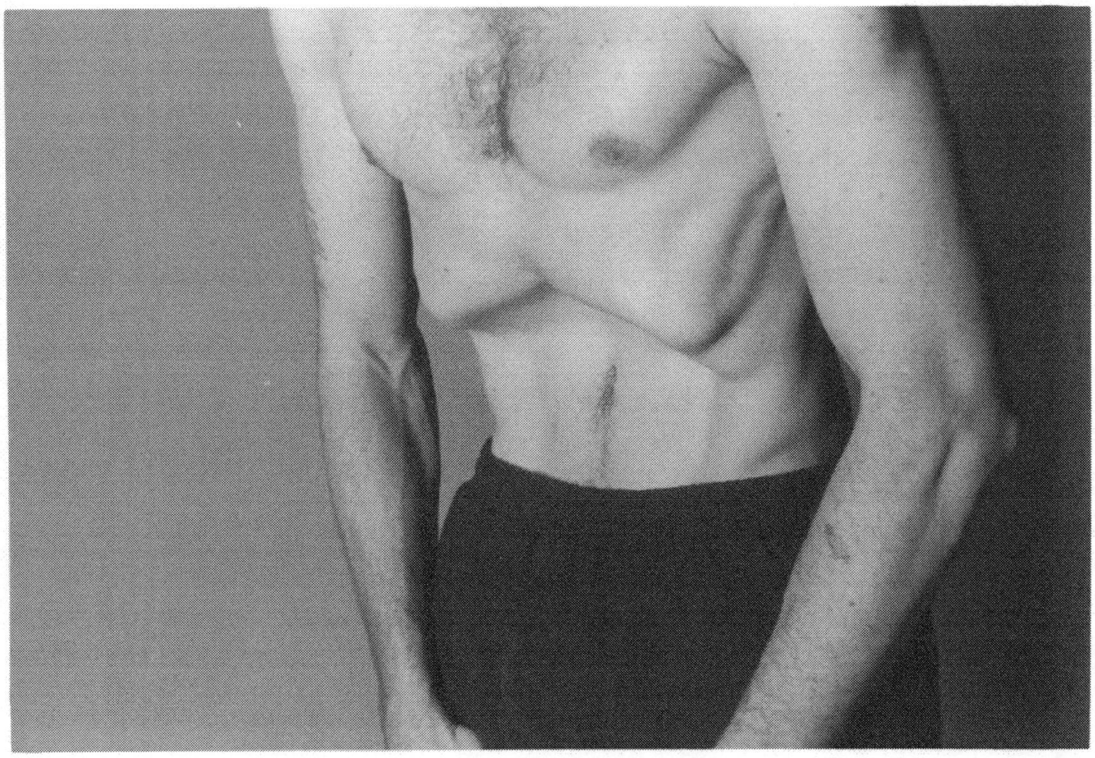

Here is a more advanced movement for **after** you master drawing-in-the-abdomen and the stomach isometrics. First, while sitting, kneeling (easiest) or standing, draw in your abdomen as in the drawing-in-the-abdomen exercise. Then bend over at the waist and push down on your thighs for six seconds. You should notice that a column of muscle sticks out while the sides of your gut draw inwards. The first few times it is likely to feel quite strange and may take some getting used to, however, with regular practice you can do it almost anywhere.

BASIC ABDOMINAL WORKOUT

Sequence

The following routine is very basic, simple and most effective when you work out the abdominals in the sequence I have provided here:

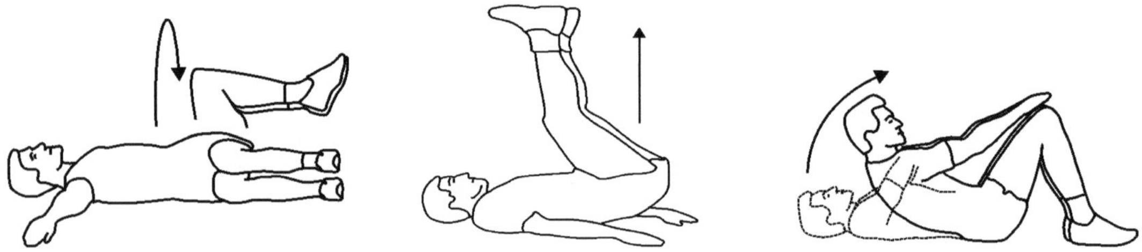

1. First, work the obliques. As these are the body's stabilizers, they will tend to assist the other abdominal groups during an abdominal workout. You will want to tire them out so that the other abdominal groups get more work. Side-to-side movements, such as leg-overs will work this area.

2. Next, work the lower abdominals. As body builders, athletes and formerly pregnant women can tell you, this is a soft area of the body that is difficult to strengthen. Movements such as leg raises will work this area. Again, you want this area pre-fatigued so that you can really work the next stage.

3. Now work the crunch for the upper abdominals. With the other abdominal groups already fatigued, the upper abdominals have to take on most of the workload. This is like most of a rowing team suddenly stopping and leaving two members to keep rowing. The upper abdominals get far more work than if they were cruising along with the rest of the abdominal "crew".

For optimum training, there should be no more than three seconds in between exercises. Otherwise, each subsequent group of abdominal muscles will recover and end up "sharing the load" with the other abdominal groups. This means less work and less results. It is better to do less repetitions, with NO rests in between, than perform more repetitions, but have long rests in between sets. The no rest method means more work for each set of muscle groups, but also superior results in less time.

If you are a beginner, start with one set of 3-5 repetitions of each movement and work your way up to three sets of 20. Then, and only then, should you increase the difficulty of the exercise. Remember that the objective here is to improve your life, not shorten it.

If you already have an abdominal routine, try to perform it following this sequence. That is, first do your oblique exercises (side bends, jackknifes, twists) second, do your lower abdominals (hanging leg raises, frog kicks, reverse crunches) and finally, the upper abdominal exercises (crunches, pull-down crunches, machine crunches). If you are doing several sets of each exercise, try instead to follow the mentioned sequence, rest for a minute and then do the sequence again. You might find yourself tiring out much quicker than with a standard routine of three sets of each exercise.

Before I learned of this technique, I used to follow the sequence backwards with fair results. Then a friend from a national cycling team taught me this sequence of working the obliques, the lower and then upper abdominals. Although I found that I was exhausted the first few times (and subsequently somewhat embarrassed), I had fast results within four weeks. And even though I was training by running and kick-boxing five days a week, I was only training my abdominals using this system, *once per week.* Within three weeks, I was seeing better results and had a faster recovery time. Most people get good results from training their abdominals three times per week.

EXERCISES

When it comes to developing strong abdominal muscles, learning to do the exercises correctly can make all the difference in the world. The benefits of a few correctly performed exercises far outweigh those achieved by performing a large number of sloppy ones. In fact, too many repetitions will actually exhaust the body to the point where it cannot rebuild itself and too much too soon is counter-productive. It is like the people who have never run more than five miles in their life and they suddenly decide to run a full 26 mile marathon. Talk about setting yourself up for failure. I knew one lady who did this and had to be taken away in an ambulance.

This is not to tell you to slack off. Just be sure to pace yourself and build up to where you can do the exercises in good form. If you haven't participated in much physical activity in the past ten years, then you have to be realistic and take it slow. Is it going to hurt in the beginning? Most likely it will, as your underdeveloped muscles get used to working again you can expect some aches and pains. So approach it like eating an elephant: one bite at a time.

For quick results, try this basic routine three times per week.

Leg-Overs

Leg-overs are good for training the obliques. To begin, lie on your back with your arms spread out at right angles to your body. Now begin to swing your legs from side-to-side, exhaling each time you swing a leg towards the middle and inhaling as your leg touches the floor on either your left or right side. Work up to 20 repetitions before increasing the difficulty level: Lie on your back with one leg straight out on the mat and the other leg towards the ceiling.

Beginner Level: Swing only one leg side-to-side at a time.

Intermediate level: Bend your knees up to the ceiling and lower both legs over to one side. Touch the floor (no resting) and raise your legs back over to the other side.

Advanced level: Straighten both legs towards the ceiling. Lower your legs to one side, then to the other.

Reverse Crunch (Hip Raise)

The reverse crunch is a good bet to target the lower abdominals. To begin, lie on your back with your arms by your sides and pressed downward against the mat. Cross your ankles, aim your feet towards the ceiling and take a healthy breath. As you exhale, raise your hips off the floor and hold the position for a couple of seconds before lowering the hips back down to the mat. For a stiff back and tight hamstrings, you might have to prop up your hips with cushions or a folded mat or lie on an abdominal board with your feet elevated.

For maximum results:

- Press the small of your back into the mat BEFORE you raise your hips off the mat. **This is important, as it will lessen the chance of back injury**.
- Keep tension on your abdominals by NOT resting between movements. Lower your trunk until it just touches the mat and then raise your hips back up again. This way, you get more work done in less time.

Beginner Level: Keep your knees bent (crossing your ankles is optional) and lift your hips so that your tailbone leaves the mat. Slowly lower back to the mat.

Intermediate Level: Straighten your legs towards the ceiling and raise your hips so that your tailbone clears the floor. Then, slowly lower your hips back to the mat.

태권도
세계태권도연맹
CAMP
PILATES
STEEL BACK
N° 6-PACK
能

Advanced Level: Legs pointed towards the ceiling and arms firmly at your sides pressing into the mat. Raise your legs, hips and lower back up to the ceiling and hold for two seconds before lowering your hips to the mat. When you raise your lower body, most of your weight should be on your shoulders and upper back.

The Crunch

Known by many, hated by a few…the crunch is a good, safe method of training the upper abdominals. Start out lying down with your knees bent and feet flat on the mat. There should be about a fist's width of space between your knees. **Press your spine into the mat** and cradle your head or just reach with straight arms and curl your upper body forward until your shoulder blades clear the mat. Exhale on the way up and inhale on the way down.

To really make each movement count:

- Squeeze the abs and exhale fully when you curl forward and up. Imagine that you are trying to crush a basketball between your rib cage and hips.
- DO NOT rest your shoulder blades on the mat between repetitions. Instead, just barely touch the mat and curl up again, so as to keep tension on your abs.
- Keep about the width of a fist between your chin and chest to avoid straining your neck.

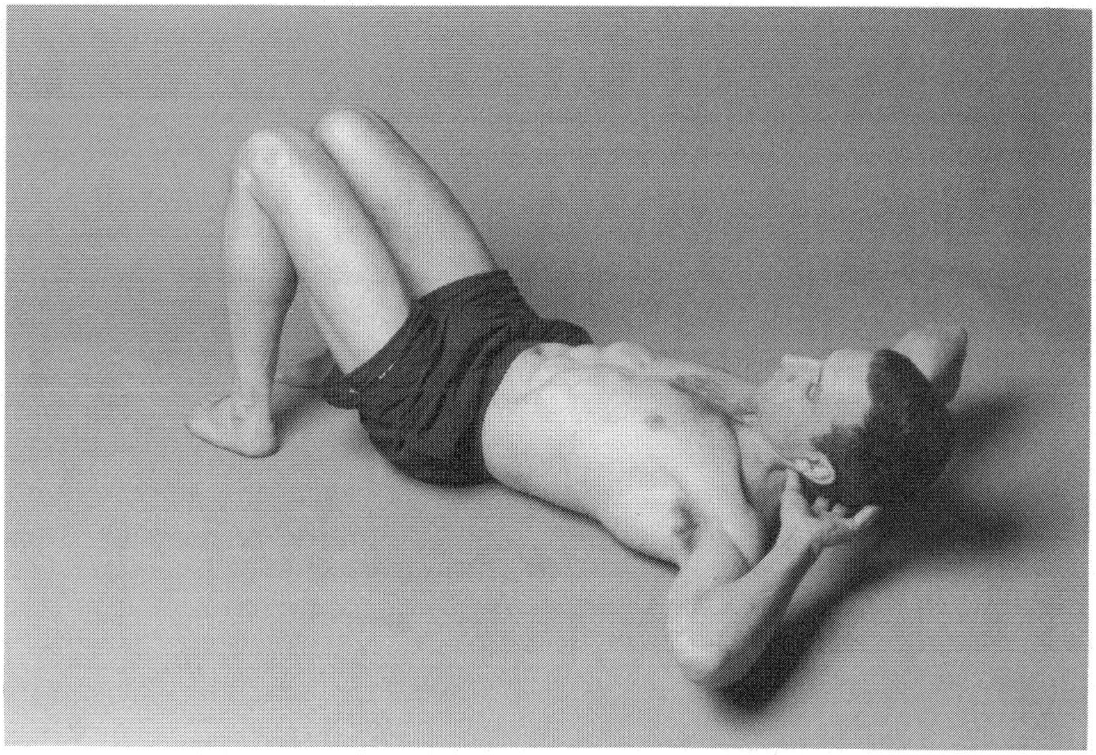

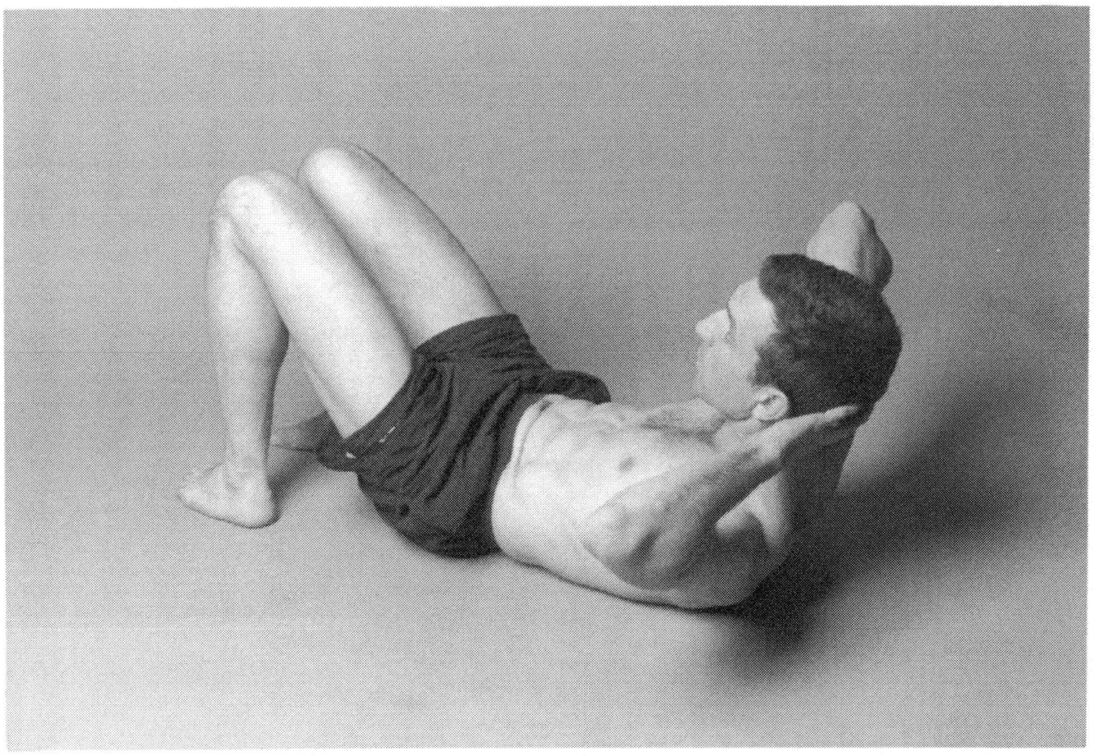

Variations

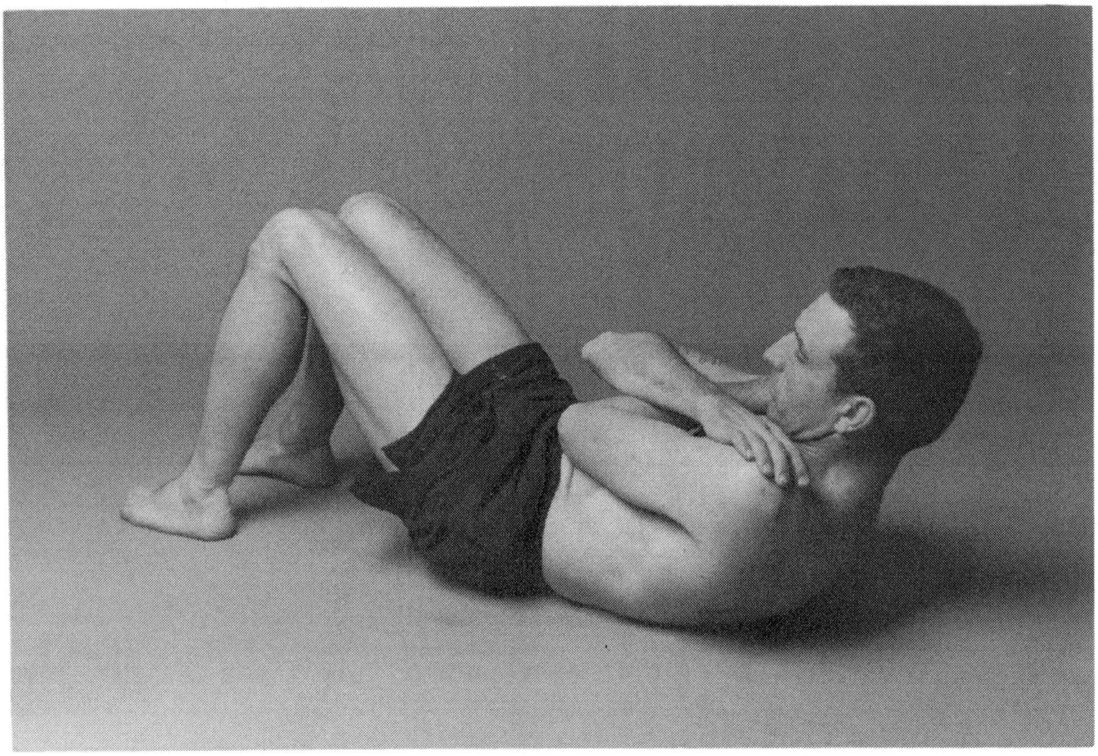

1. Hold your arms across your chest and raise your shoulder blades off the mat. Perform 20 or more micro-crunches (less than an inch at a time). This is great for ending the abdominal routine.

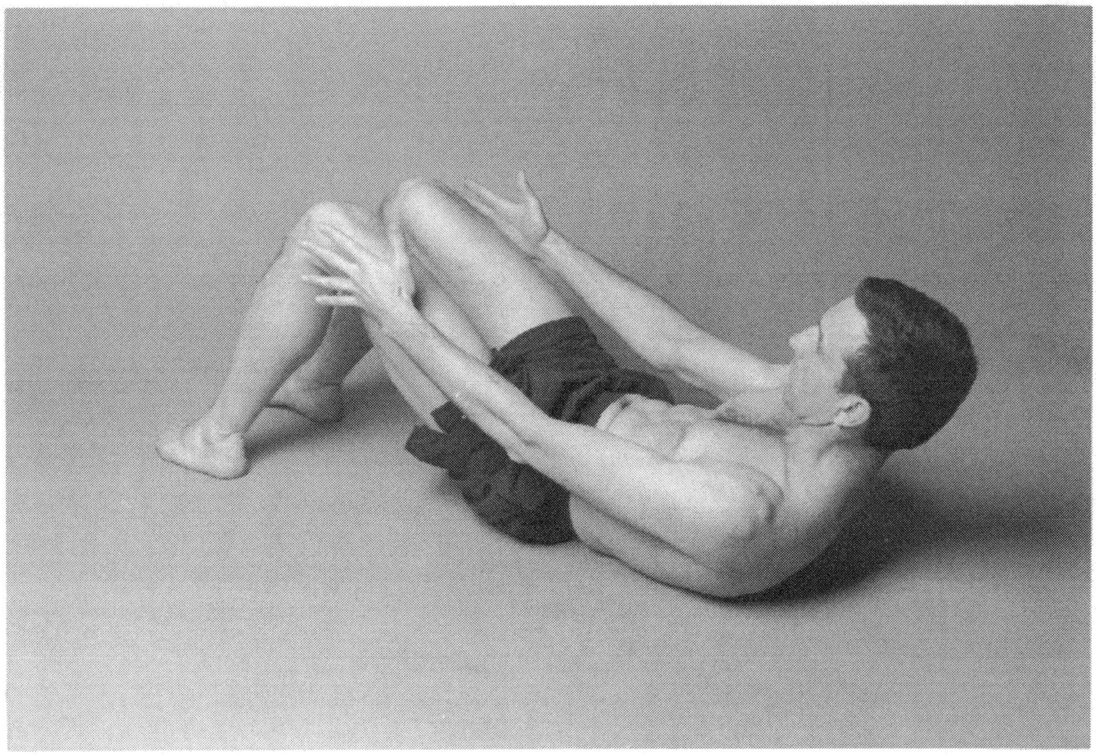

2. While lying on your back with knees raised, look at the top of your knees and extend your arms while lifting your torso off the mat. As you raise your shoulder blades from the mat, reach for the outside of your knees.
3. [Not Shown] While lying on your back, prop your legs up on a chair, a bed or up against a wall. With your hands facing palms down, slide your hands up towards your knees as far as you can go. This inverted position will take pressure off your back and give your leg arteries and veins a rest from working upwards all day long.

Please remember that even crunches can be futile if they are performed in a sloppy manner. A prime example is a heavyset guy I observed at a gym who was just butchering the crunch exercise. While lying on his back, he would slam his butt into the mat to bring his shoulders up and then ram his shoulder blades back on the mat. He did this while holding a newspaper (that he was attempting to read) up in front of his face. Where is a camera when you need one?

For good results, you have to concentrate on your workouts. Read the paper afterwards.

LOWER BACK

Beginners who are in a hurry to develop a big chest and flat abdominals will tend to neglect working their upper and lower backs. This is a problem because too much of the wrong abdominal work, coupled with not enough lower back exercise can give you an imbalanced posture. The gym is a good place to go if you want to see what over-developed abdominals look like. They often appear like lumps of rock under people's t-shirts. Although it might be solid, it can also slouch the body forward, giving a person a bent-over appearance.

All abdominal workouts should include at least a few lower back exercises and the benefits are more than worthwhile. For not only will back exercises strengthen your core area, they also tighten up and enhance your overall physique and in many cases, give you a firmer butt in the process. Two simple lower and upper back exercises are the superman and the dolphin flex.

The Superman

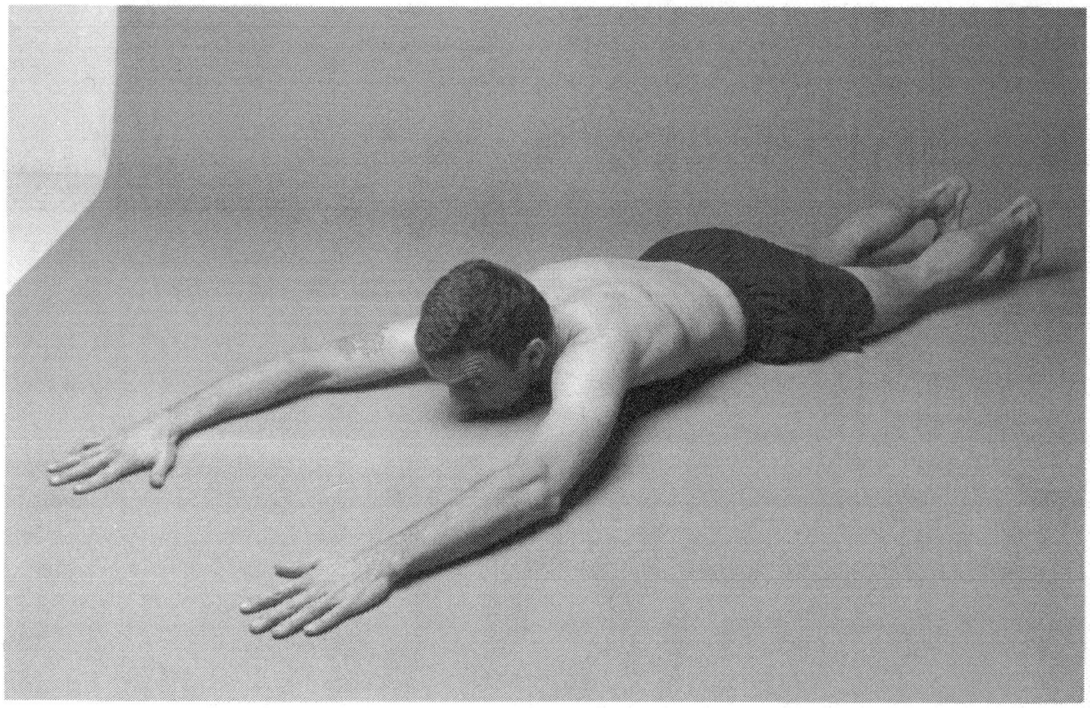

This exercise is very simple; however, you should concentrate on performing it slowly. To begin, lie on your stomach and inhale deeply. Now, raise all four limbs off the floor while reaching outwards and exhaling slowly for a count of four. You should *keep your neck straight by looking forward about a foot in front of you.* Return to your starting position and repeat. Work up to ten repetitions per set.

Dolphin Flex

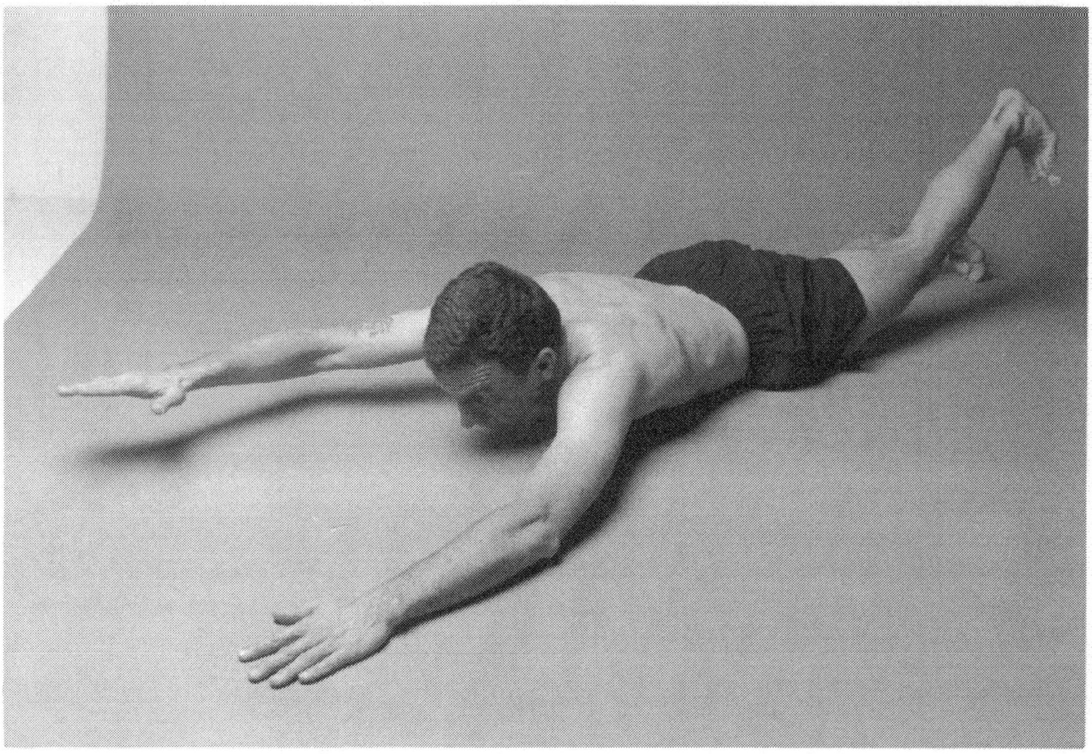

The Dolphin Flex is also known by many people as "swimming". To begin, lie on your stomach and (as with the superman) raise all four limbs off the mat. While keeping your hips on the mat, raise the right arm and left leg at the same time that you are lowering the left arm and right leg and then alternate, raising the left arm and right leg while lowering the right arm and left leg. This will produce a fluttering, swimming effect. You will find out in a hurry if you are raising the arm and leg on the same side of the body as you will tend to fall over. As in the superman, keep your neck straight by looking about a foot in front of you.

ADVANCED TECHNIQUES

When you want to test you abdominal and upper body strength, try the following gymnast positions.

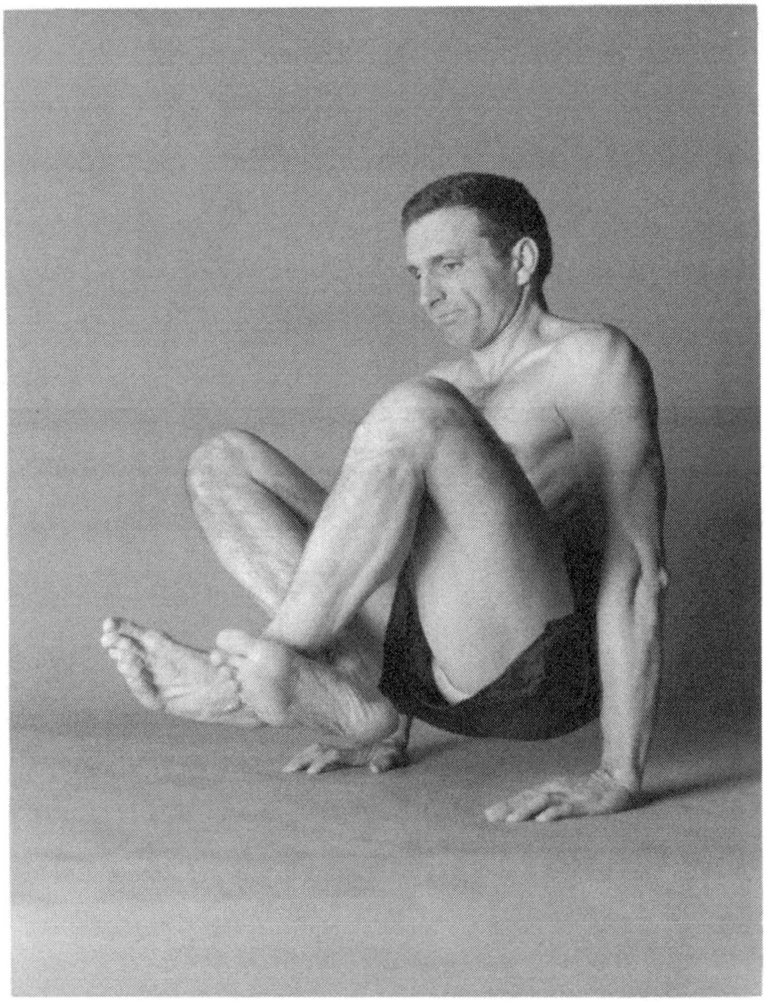

- Cross-legged L-Seat. Sit on the floor, with your legs crossed and raise yourself off of the floor while supporting all of your weight on your hands. At first, you might not even be able to move, but after awhile, you should be able to clear the ground for a few seconds at a time. Try this three or four times per week until you can hold the position for about ten seconds.

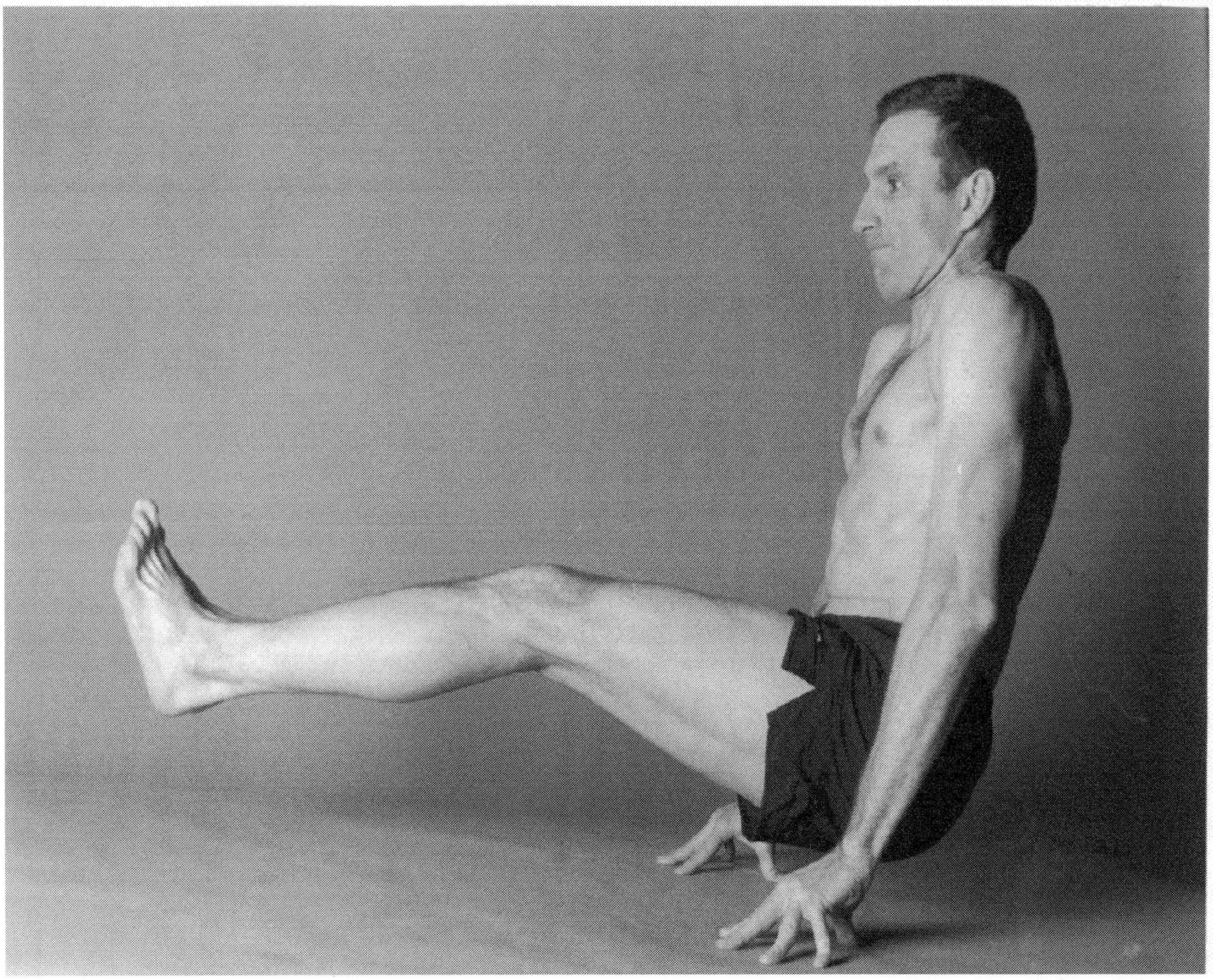

- Basic L-Seat. This is a nice little personal test to check up on your own upper body strength. To begin, sit with your legs straight out in front of you and arms by your sides with palms flat on the mat. While pushing down with your hands and tightening your abdominals and hip flexors (muscles that raise your legs forward), lift your whole body off the floor. Start out with the legs bent and progress to straight legs. A friend of mine used to do this exercise with a ten pound dumbbell on his lap.

OUTSIDE THE GYM

There is a popular belief that exercise outside of the gym is a waste of time. Try telling that to one of my lady clients who was a plumber. You might also try explaining that to miners, construction workers, cowboys, and most of the world's armies and elite fighting forces. This gym security blanket ties in with the "all-or-nothing" mentality. Some people insist that they cannot have a decent workout unless all of the high tech equipment is there in front of them. Therefore, they will either train in a perfect setting or not train at all.

Fortunately, where there is a will there is a way. Take for instance, Karen Hulse, a Women's Pro Fitness Champion. Aside from competing, she travels frequently in her work as a sales representative. When unable to get to a gym, Karen works out with rubber bands in addition to doing push ups and dips.[viii] When I was with the United Nations peacekeeping force in Croatia (former Yugoslavia), we often had no access to a gym or exercise equipment, but that didn't stop us. Working together, we came up with improvised equipment using sand bags, scrap metal and whatever else was available.

Regular workouts at the gym usually happen only in a perfect world. Since you cannot always make it to your favorite hangout, you sometimes have to look for exercise opportunities wherever you can find them. Your only limitation is your imagination.

AT YOUR DESK

Here are several micro-toners that you can do at your desk. Try these just before a break or when you start to feel sluggish.

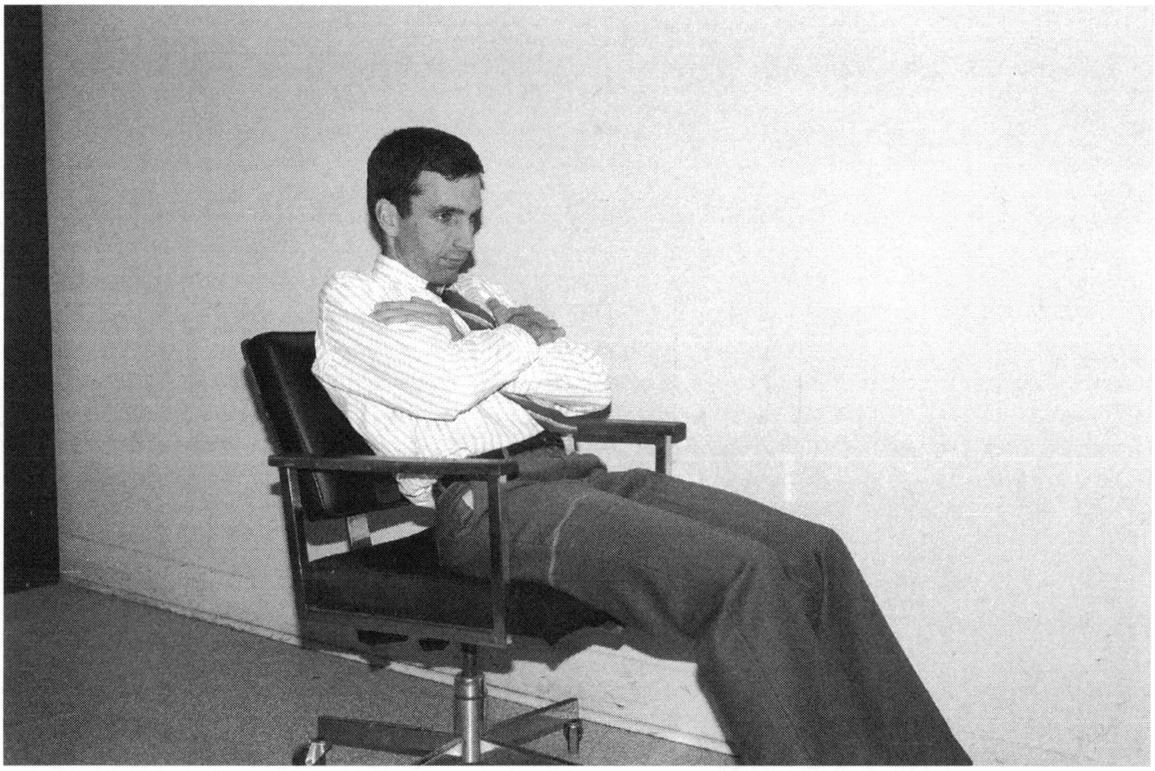

1. The Seated Crunch: [Photo] If you have a reclining back chair, you can perform this by leaning back as far as you can. Otherwise, you have to shuffle up to the edge of your seat before doing the crunches.

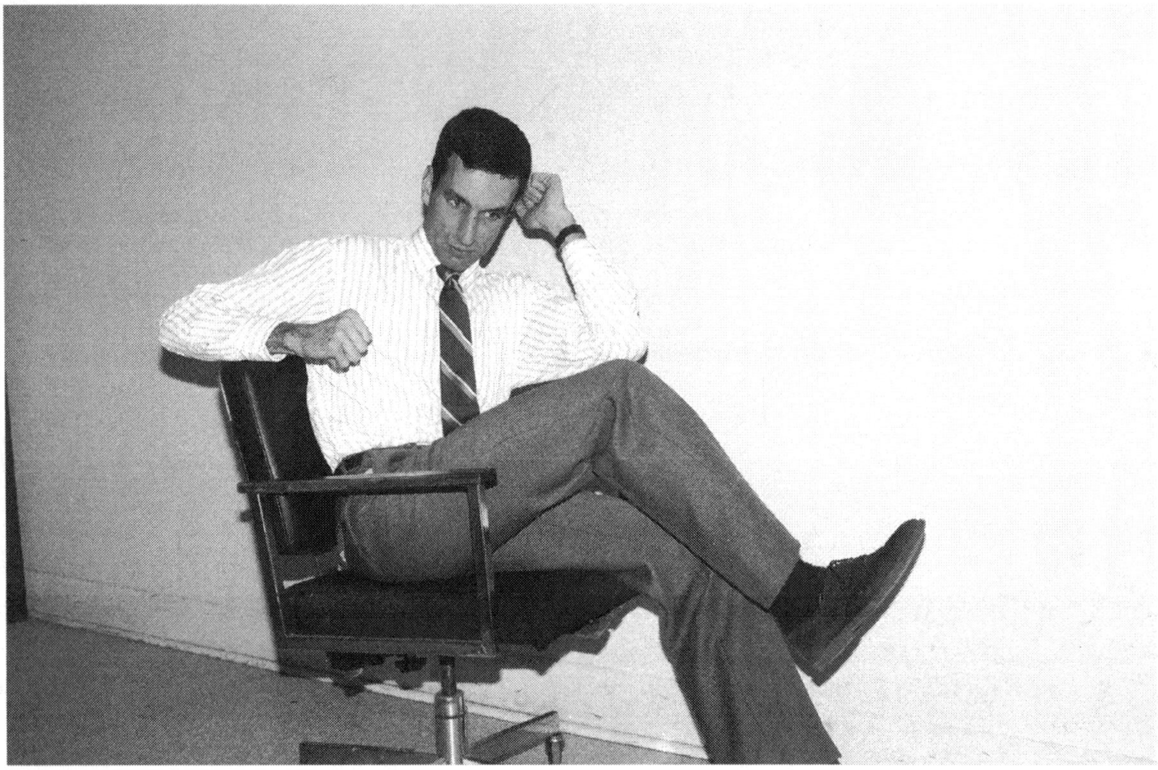

2. Cross Crunch: Lean back in your chair to put some tension on your abdominals. By just alternating the raising of your knee to the opposite elbow, you can work out your lower abdominals and obliques.

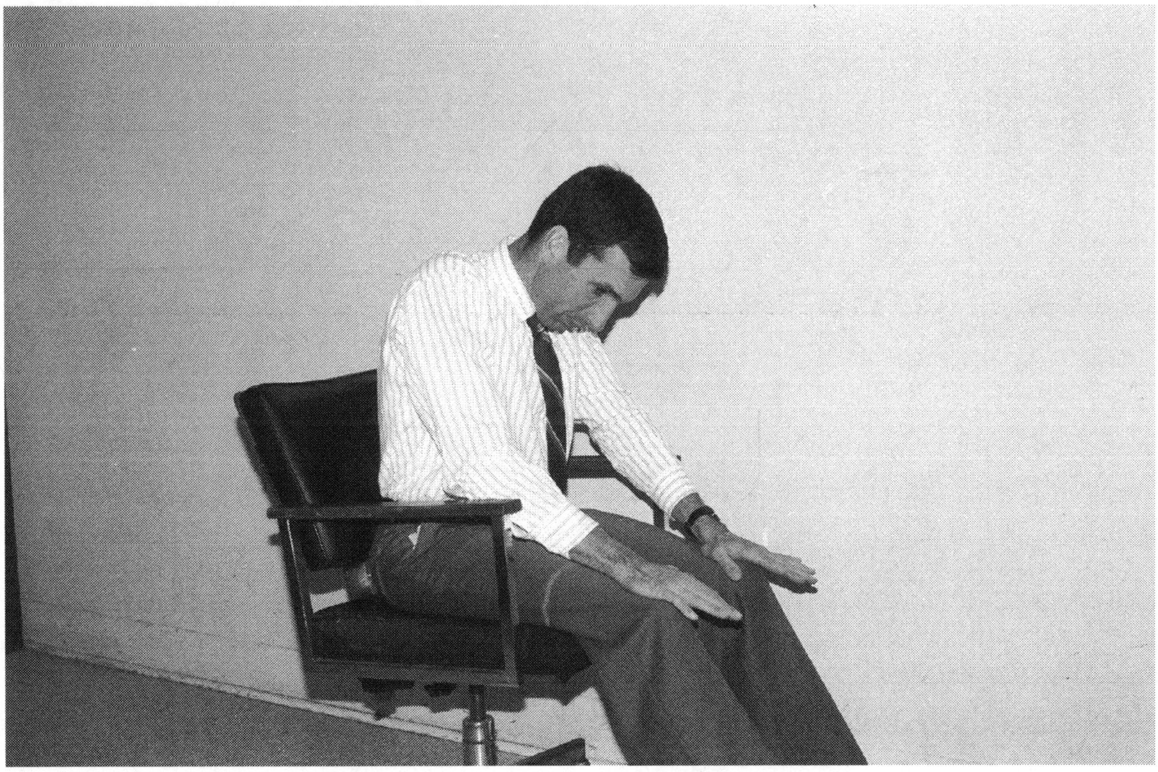

3. Isometric Crunch: While seated, take a deep breath and exhale while pushing down on your thighs or knees. Hold the position for about six seconds at a time. Ensure that you do exhale. You can also push down with your forearms to get more of a deeper crunch.

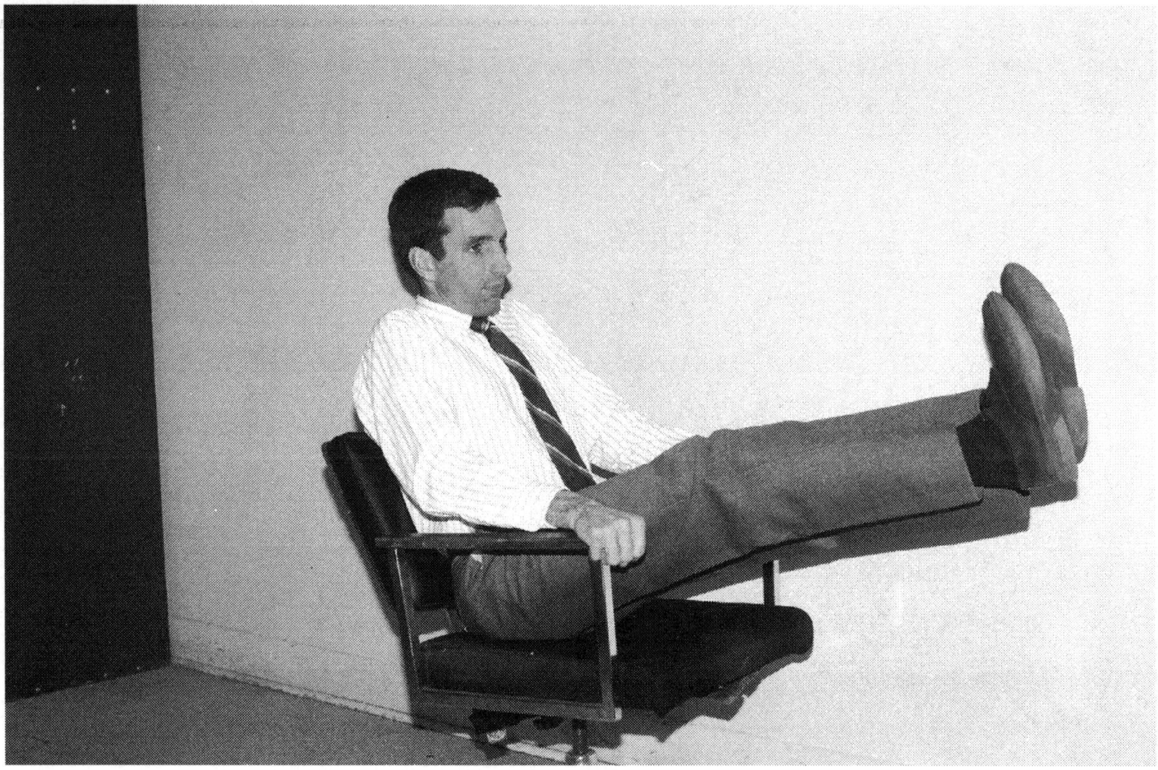

4. Leg Raise: Lean back in your chair until you feel tension in your abdominals.

   Start by raising your knees and progress to raising your straight legs off the floor.

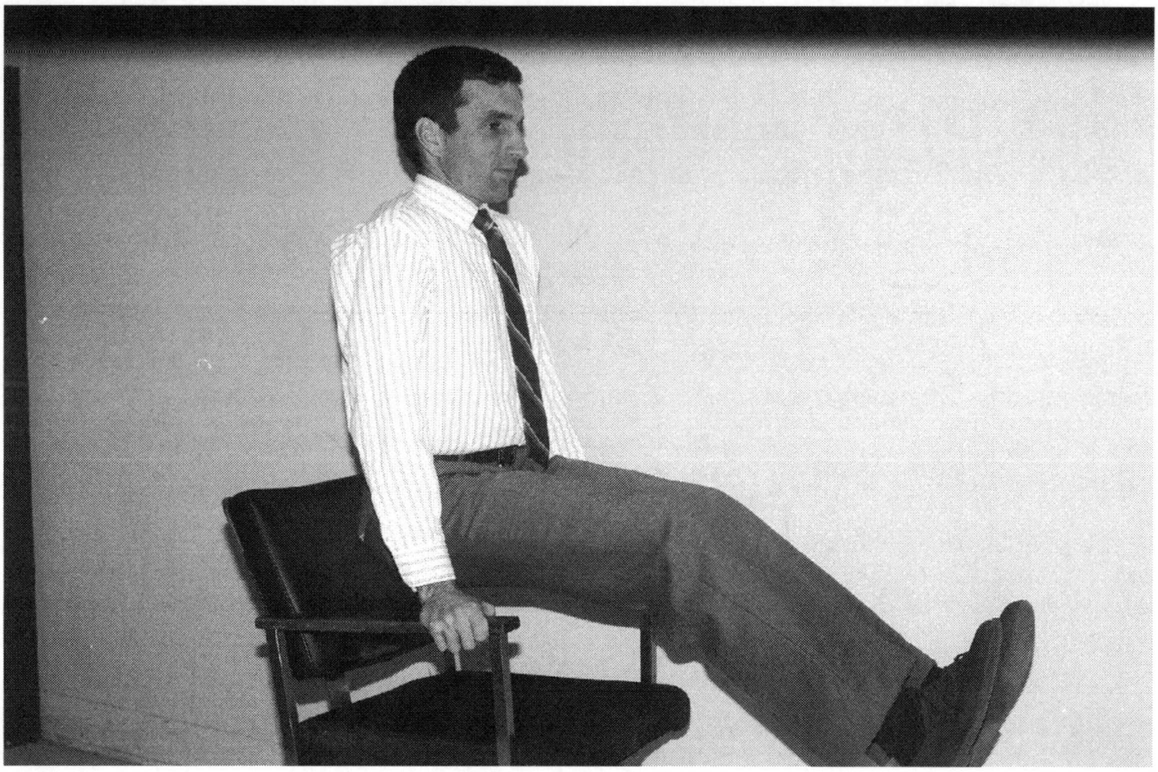

5. The L-Seat: If you are ambitious (and warmed up), you can try supporting yourself with your arms and perform the previously mentioned L-Seat.

KICKING FOR A SLIMMER GUT

According to the American College of Sports Medicine, activities that "strengthen the abdominals and stretch the hamstring muscles" can lessen back problems. This is why martial artists, who train in kicking styles such as tae kwon do, hapkido and tang soo do, will have unusually strong abdominal muscles. I have personally met people who were able to strengthen their midriffs and overcome back pain just by practicing martial arts kicking. As a supplement to, or a break from, calisthenics, kicking is an interesting method for developing abdominal and leg strength, balance and flexibility.

Front Kick

The front kick will mainly develop lower abdominal, butt (gluteus maximus, medius and minimus) and thigh (quadriceps) muscles, as well as the hip flexors. For a front kick using the right leg, start with your left leg forward, slightly bent. Keeping your balance, bring your right knee up to your chest and thrust your foot forward. The kick must be a thrusting motion to go through something, rather than a punting motion like kicking a football. For added strength, balance and muscular development hold the kick out for one to two seconds before returning your foot to the ground.

Side Kick

The side kick will mainly develop the obliques, butt and thigh muscles. For a right side kick, shift weight onto your left foot. Pivot on the ball of the left foot, so that the left heel is pointed to the right, in the direction of your kick. Bring your right foot up to your left knee and kick out with the edge of your right foot. Your upper body should almost be backwards to the target. It should feel almost like a back kick, but with your foot turned sideways. Most beginners extend their toes towards the target. This is wrong. By forcing the edge of your foot towards your target, you will get a more solid kick and better leg and butt development. If balance is a problem, begin by holding onto a stationary object such as a wall.

Once you have the knack of kicking air, try kicking a heavy punching bag without losing your balance, (falling on your butt and losing the respect of your peers). Try it. It looks much easier than it is. If this kind of activity suits you, try a few months at a reputable martial arts club and get a flat gut while learning new skills.

Running

Regardless of what anyone says, running remains one of the fastest and simplest ways to build stamina and get lean and while it is not the most exciting activity, it provides good results. Success at running is largely a mental process. I used to watch army recruits moaning, griping and faking injuries to avoid a simple morning run. Yet, during time off, the same moaners could have set records the way that they stampeded into town for a little R & R, with or without their canes or crutches.

When it comes to running, the biggest hurdle for many people, beginners and athletes alike, is to actually get out there and do it. When you start to feel fatigued or bored, a good trick is to focus on an object up ahead such as a mailbox and tell yourself that you can make it just to that object. When you reach that object focus on another object and run to that. By the time you're done, this series of short distances can add up to a good healthy run. However, even if you only make it to the end of the street, congratulate yourself for just getting outside and doing it.

I've noticed that some exercise routines insist on running a certain distance a few days per week and then gradually adding more distance over time. I prefer to just cover a certain distance with a combination of running and jogging. Eventually, I find that I am running more and walking less until I can run the complete distance.

After you can shuffle a few kilometers (miles), try a few wind sprints. A series of wind sprints every now and then will build greater muscular endurance than just jogging along at a mediocre pace. The sprinting action will also help trim the obliques and "handles" in the process. If you look at photographs of marathon runners and sprinters, you will notice that many distance runners are hard and sinewy, but also have "handles" on the sides of their waists. In contrast, sprinters' bodies tend to be more muscular overall, especially around their waists.

When it comes to sprinting, there are a few different options. One method is to run a certain distance at a good clip for a set distance, like 100 meters, then jog or walk for 100 meters. Another method is to run hard for a certain time, like one minute and then jog or walk for one to four minutes. If you are running full out for one minute, then you need about a four-minute recovery. If you neglect a proper recovery, your speed will suffer.

If you really want to give yourself a good thrashing, try this routine. Begin by running hard for 400 meters or a full minute. Next, do push-ups, squats or your abdominal routine. Finally, jog for 400 meters and then repeat the sequence three more times. This routine is sure to crank up your metabolism and harden your abdominals. Although you are sure to be sucking wind when you're done, you'll also be waaaaaay ahead of those folk who just shuffle along at a mediocre pace month after month.

There are other ways to optimize your performance as well. If you have the time, run for distance one day and then for speed another day every week. During the rest of the week, go on lighter, easier runs. By following this plan while in the army, I was able to far outdistance the guys who jogged/ran three miles a day, every day. They were not working both the slow-twitch and the fast-twitch muscles, so they were not developing the extra power. They were also trotting along at that same happy moderate pace every day so they were not challenging their bodies to go faster.

If you are planning to run, before you get out there take the time to ensure that you have good fitting running shoes and then avoid running on pavement. Running on concrete or pavement is like tapping your heels and spine with a sledgehammer, it is hard on your body, especially your joints. Instead, restrict your runs to rubberized tracks, sand, grass, bark-mulch or even gravel. It might be wetter and dirtier than pavement, but you will run longer and feel better.

Also, remember to start out gradually. I have known too many people, (including yours truly) who have run beyond their capabilities and then spent several weeks recovering from injuries rather than increasing their training gradually. Listen to your body.

SKIPPING

Skipping is a fantastic physical conditioner. A few minutes of skipping is equivalent to four times the exertion of jogging and rope jumping will also burn more calories than most other aerobic activities.[ix] Best of all, getting started is simple. To find the ideal length of skipping rope for your height, stand on one end of the rope and hold the other end overhead as far as you can comfortably reach. This measurement should give you enough room to skip while you turn the rope. Ideally, one should skip on a wooden floor and wear good running shoes to lessen the shock on the body.

When jumping rope, remember to keep your hands in close to your hips as you skip. At first, you may notice that the whole building shakes. However, as you get better you will develop a steady rhythm and lightness on your feet and as your coordination improves, the skipping gets easier. Start with one-minute sessions, twice a week and work up to three times per week. If your ankles get tangled in the rope, just jog or shuffle in place to get your rhythm back before skipping again. When you can skip at around 180 rotations per minute for three, 3-minute rounds, consider yourself in fairly good physical condition.

CYCLING

Many people in Europe and Asia use bicycles as their primary means of transportation. Here, in North America, there is something embarrassing and even dangerous, about peddling around town on a non-polluting, free-to-park machine. Yet bicycles are a very convenient way to get some exercise in whether you are shopping, commuting or out for a relaxing Sunday cycle. The price of a bike can also be less than the cost of driving your car for just one month and it is a healthy way to physically unwind from the stress of work. As an added benefit, the raising action of your legs cannot help but give the abdominals a workout.

WALKING

While it is not a big muscle-builder, walking is highly underrated as an exercise. Walking is a great way to cool down after exercising, a healthy social activity and the perfect way to end a stressful workday. It is also an easy way to relieve minor injuries, boredom or fatigue and a morning walk is a great way to wake up and start the day.

Unfortunately, over the years I have observed a steady decline in the walking ability of teenagers and young adults. Amongst basic military recruits, more than one third of all injuries are the result of weak knees and ankles (walking is the best way to strengthen both of these) and while many recruits have athletic ability, most have had little experience walking for extended periods. I find this disappointing as walking is one of the easiest and most cost effective ways of maintaining good physical and emotional wellbeing. In fact, if you live or work in a high-stress environment, consider working a light stroll into your regular routine to mellow out. After all, who ever heard of "walking rage".

Chapter 5: THE NUTRITION TRAINING TABLE

You are a custom made organism. This means that the diet that works for a pop singer, professional athlete or someone on a remote island is not necessarily going to work for either a high school student or a middle-aged desk jockey. Just because millions of Northern Asians thrive on brown rice, does not mean that someone from a South American or European background can do the same. The same goes for cabbage, high-protein, low-calorie or many other diets. Humans have evolved and adapted over thousands of years to the specific conditions and food sources in their region of the world.

Finding the diet that best suits your body's needs can be a challenge. I have seen a wide range of results from people consuming high protein, vegetarian and various cleansing diets. Some people thrive on high protein diets, while others clearly do not. Many times, the dietary needs of your body change over time. Naturopath Dr. Logan Sisk was a strict vegetarian for many years before turning to eating mostly meat. I once read about the Arctic explorer Vilhjalmur Stefansson and his two colleagues who were stranded on floating ice for several months and ate nothing but polar bear and seal.[x] According to the "experts" who follow the national food guides, Stefansson could not have survived.

I have known some vegetarians who were physically fit and strong and others who were weak and sickly. I also once met a fruitarian who was 21 years old. Although she was pretty and had the clear complexion of a 12 year old, she also had *the build* of a 12 year old.

When I ate strictly vegetarian, I noticed that I needed less sleep, but felt physically weaker. These days I include some animal protein every day. I also used to eat eggs, half a dozen at a time. Though my cholesterol was always low, I began to get nauseous and feel sluggish. After some experimentation, I found that I feel the most energetic if I only eat eggs a few times per week.

If you are going to follow one kind of diet, it is important to know what you are doing. Take a close look at the people you know who are on the diet already and how their lifestyle relates to your own. Then try the diet for a few days and note the changes in your body and mood. When you become healthier, your body will actually crave certain foods and reject others and you will start eating when you are hungry and not out of boredom.

EATING FOR ENERGY

High protein, some fats (fish oils) and high *complex carbohydrate* diets have worked for several of my clients. However, in most cases if you simply try to eat regularly and stay clear of dairy, wheat and sugar, you will find that you can keep your energy levels fairly high. Being human, I still have the odd beer, ice cream or cheesecake. This is why I will talk about guidelines, so that you can have some kind of flexibility and still have a life. That way too, you don't need to worry about a guilt trip if you occasionally "fall off the wagon." Most people can eat the following:

PROTEINS	**FATS**	**VEGETABLES**
Beef	Butter	Green vegetables
Chicken	Almond butter	(broccoli, cabbage,
		celery, lettuce,
Turkey	Olive oil	Brussel sprouts, etc.)
Fish	Sesame oil	Orange/red vegetables
		(carrots, yams, beets)
Eggs	Flaxseed oil	Bean sprouts
Tofu	Cashew butter	

GRAINS	**FRUITS**	**MISC.**
Brown rice	Apples	"Designer shakes"
		(protein drinks)
Millet	Apricots	Protein bars
Oatmeal	Pears	
Couscous		
Kasha	Berries	
Kamut		

Please note that just because a food is not on the list, it does not mean that you should exclude it from your diet. This is merely a guideline to nutrient-rich foods. When you eat nutrient-rich foods, such as broccoli or fish, you are saving yourself time and energy. By eating nutrient-rich foods you are giving yourself a greater energy return than if you eat low-value foods such as doughnuts or cake.

Of course, it is only human to occasionally enjoy some junk food. However, if you pay attention, you will find that the people who aggressively argue about their right to stuff themselves with low-value foods are the same people who tend to be tired, over-weight and/or generally in a bad mood. While in university, I was told by one professor that "there is no junk food". A registered dietitian (R.D.) also tried to tell me that a bagel was a "nutrient dense" (packed full of vitamins and minerals) food. Another R.D. recommended cookies and ice-cream to *diabetic* children (even the other students thought that she was talking nonsense). The lesson here is that even highly educated people can be biased with information. Some "experts" are paid to say certain things so that they or their university will receive funding. If you are suspicious of any claims, ask people who have had success with whatever the claim is. Quite often they are very unhealthy and are just repeating the same story sold to them. Rarely, do they have any athletic, nutrition or health background. I have talked to construction workers with better understanding of nutrition than university graduates.

If you are not satisfied with the foods on the given list of foods, look up other foods in a reputable nutrition book like Nutrition Almanac.[xi] You might be surprised at what you thought were nutritious foods. For instance, broccoli contains more potassium than bananas and black currents have over twice the vitamin C as oranges. Also, keep in mind that most organic foods are superior to genetically modified foods. But, "organic food" can also be outrageously over-priced.

Try to eat food that is fresh. This ensures the maximum amount of nutrients and the best taste. And while raw foods are superior to cooked foods in many ways, you still have to use some common sense. For instance, grains and many vegetables require cooking to break down the cellulose wall. Although this will result in some vitamin loss due to cooking, keep in mind that there is almost NO nutrient absorption if the grain or cellulose-rich vegetable remains hard and raw. Just try choking down uncooked rice or another grain and you will feel like you swallowed ball-bearings.

Some processed foods, such as some prepared camping foods are actually fairly good for nutrition and taste. Otherwise, highly processed foods tend to lack vitamin C and B vitamins and are also over-loaded with harmful substances such as MSG (monosodium glutamate). It serves you well to just eat food as close to its natural state as possible.

Of course, meats and food suspected of spoiling, must be cooked to ensure better digestion and to protect against parasites and food poisoning. Eating all raw food like raw hamburger or even unwashed fruit, all of the time, runs a risk of food poisoning. Gulping down foods like raw oysters is not the most sanitary habit either. The oyster does not have much of a filtration system and when you eat the whole thing, you are literally eating its wastes as well. One only has to have a few bouts of vomiting and diarrhea to be suspicious of uncooked food. Ensure that your food is clean, safe and properly stored. A good rule to live by is "When in doubt, throw it out."

If you are visiting a new restaurant, it is always a good idea to visit their washroom before eating. If the washroom is clean, then there is a good chance that the food handlers are clean. If the washroom is filthy…well, this is where the food handlers wash up after they use the toilet. Better to appear somewhat rude and leave than risk a bout of stomach cramps and the trips to the washroom all night. Besides, a bout of food poisoning will not impress your date either.

FOODS TO AVOID:

WHITE DEATH

Most sweet substances in nature such as berries and fruit contain vitamins, minerals, bioflavonoids and fiber. It was primitive people's natural craving for sweets that led them to seek out sources of vitamin C and other nutrients. Unfortunately, this same natural craving draws us to consume sweet, refined substances that lack any food value.

One of the most damaging sweet-tasting substances *over-consumed* in the North American diet is white sugar, also known as sucrose or table sugar. Not only is it highly addictive, but it actually depletes the body of B vitamins, magnesium, chromium and other minerals. This leads to tooth decay, nervousness, hypoglycemia (low blood sugar), allergies and mood swings.[xii] Depressed people are often suffering from low blood sugar and vitamin B deficiencies.[xiii] The over-consumption of sugar inhibits the immune system especially when it is consumed just before sleep.[xiv]

Refined sugar gives a person a little boost, so that they are rewarded with a small burst of energy…however, this burst is followed by a feeling of sudden fatigue. Then the sugar junkie needs another small fix to keep them going…which results in yet another drop in energy. This is why many people cannot seem to stop eating refined sweets every hour. To top it off, sugar addicts are the most unreasonable people to deal with when it comes to changing their habits.

A couple of simple methods for breaking this sugar fix are to:

1. Keep a journal of your eating habits and then try to figure out when and why you have this addiction. For example, some people eat sugared foods when they are stressed, worried, lonely or angry.
2. Start eating whole, high-fiber or high-protein foods *before* eating any refined sugar. This way your body will absorb the sugar more slowly than if you just ate

the refined food alone. Even eating fiber-rich fruit instead of refined sugar helps satisfy the craving for sweets while slowing down the absorption of sugar.

3. Exclude simple sugars such as fruit juice and replace them with more complex carbohydrates such as whole fruits, grains and vegetables.
4. Increase your intake of chromium. While not proven to lose weight and gain muscle, chromium does stabilize blood glucose (sugar) levels. Chromium can be found in: Broccoli, cheese, dried beans, chicken, calf liver and the supplements, chromium chloride and chromium picolinate.

Many alcoholics and drug abusers are also hypoglycemic. They constantly crave sweets. Part of the rehabilitation at the Health Recovery Clinic in Minneapolis, Minnesota, involves the removal of sugar from the alcoholic's diet. The other offending substance for *some* alcoholics is wheat.[xv] Which brings us to…

WHITE FLOUR

Bleached wheat flour is easy to store, has a long shelf life and is easy to work with. It is the main ingredient in bread, pastries, pizza dough and, oh yeah, paste for papier mâché. So, you can image your stomach trying to break down paste. Aside from having next to nothing in terms of nutritional value, white flour actually robs our bodies of nutrition because it impedes the absorption of nutrients from the intestines into the blood stream. Once it passes through the stomach, the flour forms a glutinous mass that sticks to the sides of your intestines and is difficult to digest. In the old days, eating crackers or dry bread was a common remedy when someone had swallowed a broken chicken bone or other sharp object. This is because it was well known that the gluten would coat the sharp object and often let it pass along without damaging the digestive tract.

As a food, white flour gives you the feeling of being full, with little actual nutritional benefit. People who eat a steady diet of this white paste usually have bloated stomachs and thin arms and legs. Most food banks give away bread, pastas, pastries and other white flour-based products. These items are cheap and plentiful, but hardly the staff of life.

When you are tempted to eat your next doughnut, Danish, croissant, cream puff or muffin, try eating something with less white flour such as an oat muffin, oatmeal cookie or date square. By cutting out, or at least minimizing the amount of white flour you consume, you will be amazed at how much better you feel within just a few days.

MILK

Many people from North European backgrounds can consume massive amounts of milk with no side-effects whatsoever. This is especially true if the milk is fresh and unprocessed. A number of famous body builders and athletes have been known to drink gallons of milk and remain physically powerful. At the same time, there are many, many more people whose bodies cannot tolerate the milk sugar called lactose. This makes most of the population lactose intolerant. As well, many people's bodies cannot break down the large milk protein.

Now before anyone starts protesting about milk and calcium, stop and ask yourself how it is that Native Americans, Eskimo, Inuit, African and Asian people were able to lead such vigorous lives BEFORE the introduction of milk. Furthermore, what other animal do you know of that consumes milk (let alone the milk of a different species) after adulthood? The reality is that most humans lose the lactase enzyme after the age of two. Do you think that perhaps nature is trying to tell us something?

Except for some fermented dairy products like cheese, yogurt and kefir, I have consumed very little milk for the past 25 years. My bones have not shattered, nor have my teeth fallen out. My sinuses are much clearer than they were in my high school years and I am sick less often.

Of course, it is hard to accept that what you have been force fed all of your life might actually be poison to you. A simple method to test milk's effects on you is to simply stop drinking it for a week and see what happens. If you have withdrawal symptoms (e.g. runny nose, sore eyes, gas, etc.) you might want to gradually stop drinking it.

CAFFEINE, NICOTINE AND ALCOHOL

The western world's three most common drugs are okay in moderation. However, anything more than moderate use acts as a double-edged sword to one's health. On one edge, these three are poisons that pollute the body and overwork the nerves. On the other edge, the stimulants suppress the appetite and are used in place of real food. Consequently, the heavy user gets weaker and weaker while trying to increase their energy by taking more stimulants.

Of course, someone is always arguing about a great grandfather or grandmother who smoked and drank heavily and still lived past 90. Maybe grandpa did drink a half gallon of coffee and moonshine and puff on his corncob pipe while plowing ten fields, every morning… before breakfast. People like him came from strong genetic backgrounds and worked hard all of their lives. With all that physical activity and a diet that included little or no processed food, they stayed healthy from other aspects of their lifestyle, not *because* of the stimulants.

If you are still not convinced of the harmfulness of excessive tobacco and alcohol use, just pay a visit to skid row in any town or city. There, you get to see close up, the effects of heavy drinking and smoking. Better yet, tour a hospital's cancer ward or the local police station's drunk tank.

METABOLIC TYPE

Just as there are several different blood types among human populations, so too are there different metabolic types. Determining your basic metabolic type can help you to better understand your body's basic needs in terms of nutrition, exercise and rest. Fast and slow metabolisms, also known as fast and slow *oxidizers* or *burners,* have been written about for decades.[xvi] In the book, *The Balance*, Oz Garcia[xvii] describes three basic types of metabolisms. You can take the test in Appendix A to determine if you are a Fast, Slow or Mixed Burner.

FAST BURNERS

Fast burning metabolisms are usually found in hyperactive people who often thrive on anxiety and irritability. They are often impatient Type A personalities who seem to have their adrenal glands stuck on high. They tend to have bursts of energy and have difficulty relaxing. The fast burner often has an addictive type of personality and displays obsessive traits or develops an abuse of drugs or even food. Fast Burners may not all be lean and active, but they are constantly looking for quick boosts of energy, usually through quick carbohydrate fixes.

If you are a Fast Burner, you probably skipped the metabolic test and are in a hurry to find answers. Fast Burners, like yours truly, burn out their mineral supplies like there is no tomorrow and have difficulty building muscle. This is why I disagree with diet pills that are mild stimulants that contain substances such as theobromide, caffeine and ephedrine. These "quick-fixes" will only tire you out in the long run.

A Fast Burner must maintain a steady flow of energy from their food. Take a typical eating pattern:

Breakfast: Coffee, toast, fruit

Snack: Coffee or pop and a donut

Snack: Coffee, muffin or donut

Lunch: Juice, yogurt, salad with dressing, bagel

Snack: Diet Coke

Supper: Chicken breast, boiled potato and pre-frozen mixed vegetables

Snack: Apple

It is painfully obvious that this eating pattern is packed with sugar at regular intervals. While it might fit the low-calorie, low-fat format, it is going to give the eater more ups and downs than a runaway roller coaster.

An effective fast-burner eating plan would be more like this:

Breakfast: Water, oatmeal, three egg whites

Snack: Peanut butter on whole grain crackers or chicken fingers

Lunch: Chicken or salmon salad

Snack: Protein shake

Dinner: Water, lean beef, stir-fried or steamed vegetables

Snack: Water, slice of turkey breast

The Fast Burner can tolerate higher amounts of fat and oil as they need the gradual release of their concentrated energy. Most fruits and fruit juices are high in fruit sugar (fructose) and should be avoided. However, vitamin-rich fruits such as apples, pears, apricots and all types of berries are okay.

When I find six small meals a day a nuisance, I try to have at least two good sit-down meals per day. I often did this while I was in the military, while working around the base. I found that I could actually make faster muscle gains by eating fewer meals, but eating those meals slowly.

Those high-speed, Type A people who are too busy to eat must discipline themselves to either prepare their meals in advance (and use plastic containers) or arrange to have two relaxing, uninterrupted meals per day. Many Europeans, like the Germans, eat like this. They have tea and some heavy bread in the morning, a huge (often two hour) lunch and then a moderate supper in the evening. If you have been to Germany, you might have been amazed as I was to see stores close, restaurants fill up and so many people just relaxing during one of North America's most frantic times of the day. Some might argue that this is a slack attitude. However, from my experience there, I would have to challenge anyone who questioned the productivity or good health of Germany's people.

If you are a very active fast burner, such as a competitive athlete, you can add more complex carbohydrates, like rice, yams or potatoes, to your diet. As for exercise, fast burners often benefit from anaerobic exercise, such as weight lifting, sprinting, team sports or even yoga. The short duration exercises help build muscle tissue and can have a more calming effect than aerobic exercise.

SLOW BURNERS

On the other metabolic extreme, slow burners tend to be easy-going, have low blood pressure and good digestion and often dislike exercise.

A typical slow burner eating pattern is as follows:

Breakfast: Two waffles with butter and maple syrup, two cups of coffee.

Snack: Apple.

Lunch: Baked potato, egg salad, roll with butter, fruit cup, coffee.

Dinner: Salad with dressing, rice, brownie with vanilla ice cream.

By now you can see the low-food value and high sugar content of most of these foods. This slow burner's energy is going to drop about an hour after every meal. Unfortunately, many of us have grown to accept that afternoon "dinner drunk" syndrome as being normal. When you eat properly, you can often go back to work feeling satisfied and alert. An effective slow burner eating plan would be more like this:

Breakfast: Two eggs, poached or over-easy, steamed vegetables, one cup of herbal tea.

Snack: Protein shake.

Lunch: Salmon salad with greens, tomatoes, olive oil and lemon juice, one pear.

Snack: Low-fat yogurt or cheese (if you can tolerate dairy) or almond butter and rice crackers.

Dinner: Chicken breast and stir-fried vegetables.

Slow Burners should minimize their fats and oils and stick to whole fruits such as apples, bananas and citrus fruits. Bananas and citrus fruits are high in potassium, which is a mineral that tends to be low in most Slow Burners. Grapefruits have been used for decades for weight loss as they tend to help kick-start a slow metabolism. Be aware that some people are allergic to citrus fruits and might react adversely to them.

MIXED BURNERS

Only about ten percent or less of the population is estimated to be Mixed Burners.[xviii] If you are one of these, you will have a fairly even flow of energy unless you "fall off of the wagon" from a steady intake of processed foods, coffee and reckless living. However, a Mixed Burner metabolism is not a free ride.

You can take food choices from the other types of burners and determine what works best for you. Sometimes you might perform more like a fast burner and others you might perform like a slow burner. You have to find out for yourself.

As for exercise, use anaerobic exercise, like weight-lifting to slow yourself down and aerobics, like running, to speed up your metabolism.

SPECIAL DIETS

There are always new and better diets out on the market. Some actually work… for awhile, but are difficult to maintain over a lifetime. If you look through an old bookstore or at the library you will find that many of the "new" diets as simply re-written old diets. For instance, there was a high protein diet described in *The Letter of Corpulence* by William Banting written back in 1864.[xix] Since then, there have been many duplicates of this concept, like Dr. Herman Tarnowner's Scarsdale Diet or The Atkins' Diet. While many of these concepts work great in theory for some people, few of them work for everyone all of the time. In the end, you have to find out on your own what works for you.

CLEANSING DIETS

On occasion, I go on a cleansing diet for a couple of days. This diet consists mostly of vegetable juices, soups and some fruits. I couple this kind of diet with regular saunas. After a few weeks of doing this every weekend or every other weekend, I often experience better sleep, clearer skin and better digestion. These short mono-diets and mild fasts can be beneficial if *they are coupled with lots of rest.* During my younger years, I tried to fast while maintaining a regime that included hard physical work. It left me feeling like a zombie. Therefore, I can only recommend cleansing diets if you are resting and getting the extra sleep necessary. Body cleaning, like house-cleaning, takes energy to do properly. Long fasts without trained health care supervision can be damaging to your health.[xx]

NON-ALLERGIC DIETS

This is a fascinating area, where certain foods can cause problems such as intestinal problems, like Irritable Bowel Syndrome, hay fever, attention disorders and even alcohol cravings. I became very interested in allergies at an early age, as I was constantly plagued by sore eyes, nasal drip (runny nose) and sneezing. I was constantly coughing and blowing my nose. I went through school with pockets full of tissue paper. It took me until age 20 to realize that dairy and wheat products were aggravating my hay fever and interfering with my ability to gain weight. As mentioned before, I felt far more alert and energetic when I omitted those foods from my diet.

Typical symptoms of a food allergy are: dark circles under the eyes (shiners), sore eyes, runny nose, fatigue, drowsiness, anger, shortened temper and accelerated pulse (sort of sounds like getting drunk, doesn't it?). These reactions may take effect anywhere several minutes or several hours after consuming the allergen. This can be a real problem if you have been eating allergic foods all of your life and simply learned to accept the conditions associated with them.

So, how can you tell if you are allergic to a food? If the offending food is new to you, the allergic reactions will tend to occur almost immediately. However, if the food has been consumed since childhood you will likely experience a bit of a *coffee-like boost right after consumption.* This will be followed by a drop in your energy level, followed by more cravings.

To test yourself for food allergies, try avoiding each suspect food separately for about a week at a time. What is interesting is that *you will tend to crave the very foods that you are allergic to.*[xxi] Removing these foods from your diet can be like an alcoholic trying to avoid alcohol. As your body cleans itself of the allergic food, it will experience some withdrawal symptoms, including intense cravings. This is normal. Usually, you can keep the cravings subdued by having a small amount of the offending food. Although the process of removing allergic foods from your diet might take some time to accomplish, it is well worth the effort for the result of feeling better and actually being healthier.

Chapter 6: Internal Health

Although few people want to hear about a bunch of (bleep) in their intestines, what they may not realize is that if their plumbing is backed-up, they are going to both look and feel ill. This is because the colon (large intestine) not only disposes of waste matter for the body (and the bacteria that accompanies it), but it also absorbs vital nutrients from the digested food that passes through it. A blocked colon cannot absorb nutrients efficiently because there is simply too much fecal matter in the intestines. Until it is dealt with, this will inhibit the absorption of nutrients and keep a person ill. While some people might argue that this bloating of the colon is just a few extra calories, one might also argue that these people are literally full of you-know-what. One of my fitness students insisted that his bloated stomach was "hard" and I suppose if you consider a water balloon hard, then maybe it was.

One of the primary jobs of the colon is to remove excess water from digested matter and compress the resulting waste for removal. Without enough water and fiber in your diet, this waste stops moving and the unpleasant result (as you may have experienced for yourself) is constipation. If you don't know, fiber is the substance that is not digested or absorbed during the first stage of digestion in the small intestine. Because it is not broken down, as the fiber moves on its way toward the colon it tends to absorb water and actually sweep out the intestines. Bran, fruits and vegetables provide good amounts of fiber.

Lack of exercise, dehydration and processed foods are the main causes for constipation and even some "instant" foods can cause problems in the large intestine. This is the great folly of protein powders as many of them will actually block up the colon. I found this out the hard way as a teenager trying to gain weight. Instead of huge muscles (like the body builder on the front of the container), I ended up with sinus congestion, a skin rash and some very unpopular flatulence.

Just as some people can tolerate certain foods better than others, so it is with protein powders. What works for a popular body builder might not work for the average mortal. It is in your best interest to ask around or try small amounts of certain brands of protein powders before investing in large buckets of the stuff.

Keeping the colon clean and happy is very important for overall health. When the body's exhaust systems is not working, the toxins start backing up into both the bloodstream and the lymphatic system. As a result, you end up with problems such as sinus congestion, headaches, allergies, acne, etc. The fact is, the body needs to eliminate and one trip to the toilet every three days is not enough. If you suffer from constipation, you might consider some alternative treatments. Massage, enemas, colonics, herbal therapy, proper eating and of course exercise, can get you moving and feeling better within a few weeks. Although over-the-counter laxatives may be readily available, in my mind most are a risky shortcut as they can irritate the bowels and deplete the body of nutrients. However, if you do need a laxative, the formulae with psyllium seeds are quite reliable as the ground seeds are high in fiber and expand to absorb a lot of water. Of course, for this reason, be sure to drink plenty of water when you use them.

Through the use of colonics, herbs, massage and proper foods, you can actually cure yourself of acne, allergies, colds, sore throats, headaches and fatigue. Removing white flour and sugar from your diet will greatly speed up your stomach flattening process. Forget the arguments about how much white bread your 104-year-old great aunt ate or being afraid of hurting the local baker's feelings. White flour plugs up the colon, period. Colon health might sound gross to some people. But, it is worth the time and effort to do some internal house cleaning and you will definitely feel better for it.

Chapter 7: Stomach Flattening Behavior

"We are what we repeatedly do. Excellence, then, is not an act, but a habit." -- Aristotle

Habits and results go hand-in-hand. This I can tell you based on my own experience and from the firsthand experience with others. While in the military, we had little privacy and there was no hiding each other's personal habits. We worked, ate, slept, washed, etc. in close proximity to our fellow soldiers. It was never a surprise that the party-goers were often flat broke before anyone else. Or that the guys who dressed and spoke well had plenty of dates. Or that the men and women who exercised frequently had more stamina and were in better physical shape than everyone else. The truth is, with soldiers as with all of us, in the areas of their lives where they put the most energy in, that's where they got the most results. There was no hiding that fact and in the end, it was never about "big efforts" either, just everyday habits practiced day in and day out.

The other thing that I noticed in the military was that people had different motivations for exercising or staying fit. The soldiers I knew personally, also had different reasons, for staying fit. Some wanted to take physically demanding training like the paratroopers or pathfinders. Some liked morning runs, while others did it out of necessity. Some were crazy about sports. One guy tried to go AWOL so he would not miss his floor hockey game. Still others just liked socializing at the gym.

Everyone has different motivators towards or away from exercising. Some children learn at an early age to link exercise with either satisfaction or disappointment depending on their experience. For some, participation in physical activities such as sports means approval from parents, teachers and peers. This is especially true in high school, where athletes often receive extra attention and special privileges. The story is quite different however, for those who were physically awkward as children. Often ridiculed while playing sports, bullied by their more athletic peers or humiliated by gym teachers, these children learned to hate anything related to physical education.

Now in adulthood, some people still feel certain resentments towards structured exercise. Some get their exercise by pursuing the social "singles scene" that is prevalent in fitness clubs. Many overstressed people, like the newly divorced, use exercise as a release to vent their frustrations. Others need the open spaces and freedom of outdoor activities like hiking, skiing or scuba diving. Still others trudge along treating exercise as a bitter pill that they have to swallow, or if they can, avoid altogether. It is this latter group that has to find a way to make physical activity a pleasant habit and lifestyle.

There are several psychological methods for changing a lifestyle. Find a method or combination of methods that suit you and stick with them for *at least 30 days*. You will be amazed at the phenomenal results from just a few subtle changes.

VISUALIZATION

Visualization is simple, yet not easy. By regularly thinking about or picturing something, you will tend to move towards what you dwell on. Either that, or the object or situation will be drawn to you. Usually people do not get what they hope for because they are *thinking about several other conflicting things*. They tend to use visualization in a negative way. It is like people actually praying for something that they want and then ending off their session with the thought, “but it’s not going to happen”. Or they focus on what they are afraid of. How many times have you heard, “I was afraid that would happen”.

Even if you are afraid of something else happening, you must keep focusing on your objective and stay positive in your visualizations. You have to look past the obstacles and keep on track with what is important to you. It is like the advice for new drivers, “keep your eyes on the road, not the ditch”. When I was trying out for the Canadian Airborne Regiment, I kept seeing myself wearing the paratrooper’s maroon beret. Despite disapproval from some supervisors and peers, I eventually got there. I used the same technique to run marathons, win kick-boxing matches and complete a university degree. Whenever, I was not focused on my goal, I often fell short or failed.

Some high performers, like top athletes and entertainers, visualize their success in fine detail. For instance, a rock-climber might picture himself on a cliff face. He is so tuned into the visualization that he can feel the cold or heat of the rock as he moves himself along, from one gripping point to the next. To complete the visualization he might imagine himself up close, making all of the right climbing moves to get to the top and conquer the cliff.

Some people find that it makes the visualization process easier if they put up pictures of the goal they are working towards (images of high-performance athletes, models, vacation spots, vehicles or houses). When they see these pictures, they tend to think about what they want and subconsciously invent ways of achieving their goals. I used to pin up photos of famous athletes that I aspired to be like. This is why a training environment is important. At the Canadian Airborne Centre, there were chin up bars and training apparatus everywhere. Most of the walls were covered with flags, graduation plaques and motivational signs such as this: "Pain means that you are still alive". As we trained, we focused on passing, not failing and most of us ended up wearing the paratrooper's jump wings.

AFFIRMATIONS

Aside from picturing what we want, we can also support our mental process by verbalizing and writing down what we want. It's true that what we focus on is what we get. So, if you keep talking about how good business is or how much life sucks, eventually it becomes a self-fulfilling prophecy because you will look for or attract elements that support what you believe. For myself, I have found that just repeating phrases like, "I can do this" over and over can help accomplish certain things when doubt has crept into the back of my mind.

Verbalizing your goals is a very useful tool provided that you:

1. Keep it simple. "50 crunches are easy".
2. Keep it positive. "I am getting stronger every day," rather than "I am NOT getting weaker" or "I am NOT a blob."

3. Keep it in the present. Dwelling on the past or "some day" isn't going to work. Goals require action now and they require deadlines.

Obviously, if you keep repeating something that you know is not true, you will not get much in the way of results. This is where writing out the idea or goal will help. However, this does not mean mindlessly writing out the statement over-and-over, like a grade school punishment. One way to find an affirmation that you can work with is to make two columns on a sheet of paper with the statement (or affirmation) column on the left taking up two-thirds of the page and the response column taking up the remaining one third of the page on the right.

Now, write a statement that you expect to be true on the statement side of the page and then write the first thing that pops into your mind on the response side of the page. At this point, it is not uncommon to find some very negative responses dredge up from your past but don't let this slow you down. You have simply reached the turning point where part of your mind is struggling to hold onto negative thoughts. Be prepared to face the thoughts, accept them and continue with your affirmations. This may be very uncomfortable at first but there is no reason to panic. Whenever a protest pops up (e.g. you can't do this, you are too old, young, weak, etc.) just thank yourself for the response and keep moving. We are doing a bit of mental housecleaning here, so don't be surprised if you find more than just dust bunnies in some of those dark corners. Just remember though, that things that hide in the dark and cast big shadows aren't nearly so scary when we pull them out into the light.

To make your affirmations even more effective, try writing your statements in the first, second and finally, the third person. Write out the affirmation five times for each viewpoint and try to write these out three times per day.[xxii]

For example,

STATEMENT	RESPONSE
(First Person)	
Working out is easy for me.	*What are you nuts?*
Working out is easy for me.	*Yeah, and there's no time for anything else.*
Working out is easy for me.	*And be anorexic.*
Working out is easy for me.	*????*
Working out is easy for me.	*Not you, geek….*
(Second Person)	
Doug, working out is easy for you.	*Says who?*
…etc.	
(Third Person)	
Working out is easy for Doug	*Sometimes.*
…etc.	

Usually, while writing these statements, there will be some strong protests. After all, most of us were told from an early age that we had certain limitations (e.g. "*You'll never do that,*" "*Kids today are so lazy,*" "*Life is hard...then you die*"). But after a few days the resistance should begin to crack, with responses like, "Well, usually working out is hard, but sometimes it's easy like last Wednesday when I ran for ten minutes without stopping." This is the point where your mind starts to give up some of those old negative beliefs and replace them with more positive ones that are based on recent experience. Of course, not every affirmation will be the same. In some cases you may find that you are facing weeks and weeks of steady resistance. If there is real resistance to a statement, try letting it go for a while and come back to it later. In the meantime, try a different affirmation.

One of the more difficult statements to deal with has been: "People want me to succeed." Try that one out for size. It is really amazing the amount of trouble or number of problems that most people have with writing out that particular phrase.

More popular affirming statements are:

I am good to my body and my body is good to me.

I am stronger every day.

I eat what is best for me.

I appreciate myself.

People want me to succeed.

Money flows to me freely and easily.

Having said all of that about affirmations, remember that not every method works the same for every individual. If you find that writing out these affirmations is too weird, awkward or unscientific for you, then please try something else.

JOURNALING

Many days you will feel like there is NO progress at all taking place. When you get in better physical condition, you will usually not recognize the subtle changes until you look at previous photographs or measurements, try on old clothes, or hear feedback from friends. This is where journaling comes in, as it is far easier to *stay on track*, if you can *keep track*.

To start journaling, you must figure where you are now. By determining your starting point or **baseline**, you give yourself a reference point. Your baseline can be made of beginning body measurements, time to run a certain distance, number of exercise repetitions or even time spent on an activity like running, swimming or cycling. A very practical method is to take your Waist-Hip-Ratio (WHR) as mentioned in Chapter 1.
To get somewhere, you must start somewhere. Even if you only walk around the block or visit a gym once a week, that is okay. Just record it.

Even the simple act of riding a bicycle to the store a few times each week is worth recording. By writing down your activities, you are actually becoming more aware of what you are doing or not doing. I do this with training, writing and studying. It only takes a couple of minutes per day to mark it on a calendar or make an entry in a notebook. Keep the journal accessible so that you have a constant reminder of what you want to accomplish. You might find too that you want to change your goals from time to time. This is important as it helps to redefine what you want and keep you pointed in the right direction (maybe you don't want a 24-inch waist after all, maybe you just want a date).

During days of unusually low or unusually high performance, you should mark down what was happening that *week.* This way, you can determine what might be helping or hurting your performance. Changes in eating, working, sleeping and your personal life will often reflect your training. For instance, if you are excessively tired on Wednesdays after working late on Tuesdays, then you should consider making Wednesday an easy training day or get more sleep on Monday night. Some people insist that they get better workouts early in the morning, especially if their jobs entail standing all day. A bit of planning can bring big results. See Appendix B for an example of a quick and easy training record.

A friend of mine, Mike Feuntespina, is a former international cyclist. He is constantly measuring his performance in martial arts, cycling or business. He looks for subtle changes in skills and strives to improve them, even if in small amounts. He watches his training like a broker at the stock market and his performance speaks for itself.

REWARD REINFORCEMENT

Maintaining reward systems or positive reinforcement is an important part of building life-long habits. As human animals, we generally like to repeatedly do the things that we have been rewarded for. The basis of positive reinforcement or habit-changing is that when someone does something and is *immediately* positively reinforced, they will tend to do the same thing again in a similar situation.[xxiii] You will note the word *immediate.* The person who plans to train and diet all year and then reward themselves with a summer vacation, has less chance of success than someone who gives themselves *small, but immediate* rewards for training and dieting, throughout the year.

The first big mistake that people make with the reward system is *delayed rewards*. Trying to get in shape for a vacation or the forthcoming summer season when it is still several months away might be a good reason to train, but it fails to motivate as a strong reward. To grudgingly drag oneself down to an unfriendly gym or pedal on an exercise bike in the corner of one's basement is just plain punishment. I recall my stepfather recovering from a heart attack by peddling on an exercise bike. He lasted about two and half weeks before resuming his usual routine of television-watching, chain-smoking and beer-guzzling after work. His second heart-attack followed a few months later, at age 46. The problem was that there was no reward linked with the daily activity. Unfortunately, there was also a hell of a punishment waiting for him as a result of his slipping back into old habits.

Frank, who is a retiree, used a more successful method of behavior modification, After failing several times at exercising, Frank put exercise into his own established routine. This original routine was: coming home, grabbing a beer and sitting in front of the television. What Frank did was come home, put on his sneakers, walked around the outside of his house once (the behavior) and then have a beer (reward). After a few days, he was walking around his house several times before sitting down to a beer. Gradually, Frank set goals of greater distances before accepting his reward. He must have really wanted that beer as he was soon jogging a quarter mile every day.[xxiv]

I cannot stress enough the importance of immediate rewards during a habit-changing program. The shorter the time span between the activity and the reward, the stronger the habit-forming bond. It is even better if you can incorporate the reward into the activity. For instance, many of my own workouts involve going to a good gym, talking to interesting people, listening to good music and sometimes, eating at a restaurant with friends after the workout. For me, this is a great reward for working out and I associate my experience at the gym with good times and good folk. However, suppose that I was in total pain throughout my workout, the people in the gym were all rude and unwashed, my locker was broken into and the restaurant food that I had later made me ill. In this case, my whole gym experience would relate to nothing but misery and chances are I wouldn't be eager to do it again anytime soon. When you start training for fun rather than just health, it becomes much easier.

The second big mistake that people make with the reward system is giving *large rewards for small efforts.* This is typical of people who believe that a couple of hours of playing sports is a great excuse to guzzle a case of beer. Another example is dieters who think that eating salad all week entitles them to eat a whole chocolate cake or go on a shopping spree that they can't really afford. Or the guy who makes a big production out of eating a few carrot sticks for supper and then heads out to the bar to knock back a few pitchers of beer because he "earned it".

The problem with large rewards for small efforts is that over time you will need increasingly larger rewards to get the same result. Some dog trainers have this problem when they only use food as a reward. The dog will eventually only respond when it is hungry. It's also like bribing a spoiled child to do anything. The rewards have to get larger and larger to be effective.

The solution to this problem is to give *consistent, small rewards for regular efforts*. So, in the case of exercising, the trainee should follow up the exercise session with small rewards like watching a favorite show, telephoning a friend or having a drink of juice. After a workout at a gym, one can schedule a walk through the mall or bookstore, a stop off at a coffee shop or whatever is routine and fun. One does not have to break the bank as part of a reward system.

The same goes for following an eating plan. By arranging the food to taste good or to take place in a good-time environment, you develop a mental link between eating healthy and enjoyment. For instance, there is probably not much fun to be had sitting home alone and eating a pre-frozen, low-calorie meal. However, if you eat that same meal at a park, during a good television movie or in good company, the meal becomes a pleasant experience. Personally, I would rather eat a hotdog in a park with friends than indulge in a gourmet meal at a high-class restaurant with company that I don't enjoy.

This method of small, consistent rewards can be applied to any regular task that you find challenging. It helped me immensely with my studies at university. As a reward for studying 15 extra minutes, twice a day, while traveling on the bus, I would get to read fiction for a designated period of time after each study session. Within a couple of months, I raised my Biology marks from a D to a B average.

Take the time to plan out your own small reward system to support your training program. A little bit of planning done now will pay off with big dividends later. See the behavior contract in Appendix C.

BEHAVIOR MODIFICATION THROUGH PUNISHMENT

Obviously, if cigarettes tasted bad or booze caused instant hangovers, there would be fewer people smoking and drinking. Punishment for bad behavior is effective, but it has its limitations. First of all, the punishment has to be immediate otherwise there is no link between the punishment and the activity. For instance, if a dog owner beats a dog for something that the dog chewed up yesterday, the dog gets confused because it doesn't really understand what it is being punished for. The same goes for beating yourself up emotionally after missing exercise or eating too many desserts. The bad feelings (or punishment) that you have after the fact, don't really link pain to the undesired action.

One way of teaching the mind negative consequences is through *avoidance conditioning.*[xxv] This is accomplished by causing some kind of mild pain during the unwanted activity. I tried this with a friend of mine who wanted to quit smoking. To help him quit, I got my friend to do 20 push ups before every cigarette he smoked. This got him pumping out push ups during every work break before he could have a cigarette. While it didn't get him to quit immediately, it did help get him into better physical condition and as the days wore on, he found more and more excuses NOT to smoke. Six months later, he did finally gave up smoking And although he quit under his own willpower, he commented that the push-up routine really had helped.

I also knew a Pilates instructor who used to mark down on her cigarette package the number of cigarettes that she smoked throughout the day. At the end of the day, she would do several pushups for every cigarette smoked. When I was trying to break a bad habit, I would do 50 or more push ups before I did the activity (like eating junk food). After a few times of this routine and I found excuses not to do the activity.

TOKEN SYSTEM

Using a token system or token economy[xxvi] is a variation of the reward system. Some of you may be familiar with the token systems used in schools (gold stars, letter grades), by credit card companies (air miles, reward points), auto insurance companies (demerit points for bad driving or discounts for good driving) and juvenile detention centers (points given or taken away based on behavior). And chances are that pretty much every one of you is familiar with the most universal of token systems…it's called money.

To use a token system, simply "pay" yourself a token every time that you perform a desired action, like physical activity or eating properly. While any kind of token can be used, I prefer to pay myself money. This way, the reward is more tangible and immediate. For instance, for every hour of studying a difficult subject or writing that I do, I pay myself a dollar an hour. I also mark it on the calendar. Then, every weekend, I use the money to pay for some type of entertainment such as a movie, book or to go out to a restaurant. Keep in mind that, like the reward system, the token must be spent soon and on something enjoyable. The amount really doesn't matter as much as the gesture. (Some people will pay themselves less than a dollar a day, while others can afford to pay themselves $50 a day). However, saving up over several months or using the money for something necessary like car repairs or a telephone bill defeats the purpose of the reward. If all that you can earn for yourself is $1.50, then make sure that you spend it on something or 'towards' something that will feel like a treat.

The token system can also be used as a punishment, just like with traffic tickets. For instance, every time that you eat junk food or skip a workout or activity session, you can give yourself a small fine. This can be a small amount of money (like a quarter) subtracted out of your reward system or a donation towards a charity. If you are competitive, you can make a pact with a friend to pay your fines to each other or pay the other's lunch at the end of the week.

One popular example of a *token system* of punishment is the decades old "cuss box". With the cuss box, whenever someone swears (cusses), they have to pay a prescribed fine, dropping the appropriate amount into the cuss box. I used this method very successfully one summer as a "sarcasm box," after a co-worker remarked that certain sarcastic remarks were coming from my end of the office. To curb this habit, I would pay the sarcasm box between ten and twenty-five cents for every sarcastic remark that I made. This helped me stifle making certain remarks…for about a week. Then, as is common with many behavior changes, I had a relapse. In fact, there was such an intense return of my sarcasm habit, that I just dropped five dollars into the box and let loose a week's worth of comments. After that the habit simply faded and at the end of the month I used the money in the box to take my co-worker out for food and drinks.

Although it is helpful to get started on new habits, eventually you will want to wean yourself off the token system. There are two effective methods. The first method is to demand greater performance (like Frank running a quarter mile, instead of walking around the house) for the same number of tokens. The second method is to increase the length of delay before the token is issued. This could mean that you give yourself a token at the end of the day or week for good performance. Personally, I keep using the token system on an on-going basis for a few habits that are just plain hard to change. If a system works for you, use it.

ESTABLISHING A ROUTINE

Ever notice how some people always have to have a cigarette with their coffee or drink? This is because an action performed with a routine activity will tend to reoccur with that routine activity. Often called the *Premack Principle,* it means developing a habit by coupling an uncommon activity like memorizing notes on a bathroom mirror, with a common activity like shaving. If done frequently enough, the person shaving will tend to start looking for study notes whenever they get to a mirror for shaving.

To apply this to our exercise routines, we want to link a regular activity with physical activity. This can be something as simple as stretching while watching television or doing pushups and crunches during commercial breaks. I once asked a very muscular 65 year old martial arts instructor how he stayed in such good shape. He answered that he exercised lots and ate lots, usually while watching television. He mentioned that once he had performed 1,000 leg raises in front of the television set.

An even simpler method is to think positive thoughts during routine activities. This could include reciting a short pep talk every time you sit down for a meal or get behind the steering wheel of your car. One psychologist had his 17-year-old college student client imagine positive thoughts just before a trip to the urinal.[xxvii] By coupling the two activities, the student automatically gave himself positive thoughts every time he went to the urinal (hopefully, the process did not reverse and make the guy lose bladder control every time he had a good thought).

In applying the *Premack Principle*, try to combine a wanted behavior with your own normal routine. This might mean doing five or ten squats before and after shaving or doing the drawing-in-the-abdomen exercise every time you get in your automobile.

DELAYING GRATIFICATION

In the military we are taught the tactic of delaying the enemy at every opportunity. This strategy also works well for fighting bad habits with the idea being that you *delay* the reward system or positive reinforcement involved with the bad habit. For instance, the simple technique of not having junk food in your home will force you to travel for it if you really want it. Another way to cut down on unwanted snacking is to put the snacks in a difficult place, like the attic or a high cupboard, to again, *delay the gratification*. Some people who have difficulty with impulse buying freeze their credit cards in a block of ice so that they have to wait for the ice to melt to make their next purchase. *Delay, delay, delay...*

When it comes to delayed gratification, even subtle activities will work. For example, you can reduce over-eating at the dinner table by putting down your utensils between bites. Aside from delaying the good taste of another mouthful of food, this can actually make you feel fuller with less food. Eating slower gives the body time to produce enough of the CCK (cholecystokinin) hormone to give you that feeling of fullness.

If you have the couch-potato syndrome, you can delay the process of coming home and going straight for the living room couch. Some people avoid slacking off by making sure that they go directly to a gym after work. Others take their children for a walk or bike ride *as soon as they arrive home*. Find a suitable delay tactic and then make it part of your routine.

If you like dessert after supper, try to further delay it by having it *after* you wash the dishes or take out the garbage. Friends of mine insist that their children clean the supper dishes and do other chores *before* eating dessert. This not only delays the reward of eating dessert, but it also provides an incentive to complete certain chores that might otherwise be put off and gives you a greater sense of control.

No one ever said that delaying an unproductive (yet very enticing) course of action is easy. For instance, I once had the dilemma of stopping for a few cold beers after work or riding home on a hot, crowded bus. As I recall, it was a sweltering prairie day and I had been replacing toilets in an apartment complex for eight hours straight. On my way to the bus stop after work, I stepped into a bar to make a telephone call. The air inside the bar was cool and filled with the sound of clinking beer glasses, music and friendly conversation. As I turned around after my call, I was faced with a difficult choice. Should I relax with a couple of cold brews until rush hour was over or step back outside into the wall of heat and board a stuffy, overcrowded bus. Did I mention that I really hated riding that Friday afternoon bus? Fortunately, for me, I had some goals to help pull me through. At the time, I was saving up money for university and I also had plans to go out that evening. As it turned out, those two thoughts provided just enough incentive to drag me away from the inviting bar and onto that cattle car they called a bus for the ride home.

To overcome moments of weakness, you should plan ahead and have some kind of reward (or punishment) system already in place, *before* you get sidetracked.

ENVIRONMENT

Planned environments, also known as *situational inducements,* can encourage certain behaviors. Grocery stores use bright displays and music to induce shoppers to buy more than they might have planned to. Fast-food restaurants use small, uncomfortable chairs to encourage patrons to eat and leave quickly.

During military parachute training, at the Canadian Airborne Center, we were immersed in a physical training environment. Everywhere you looked, there was training equipment, chin up bars and motivational signs like "Try more push-ups" and "Do more chin-ups". Of course the instructors were always nearby to provide encouragement (by yelling or commanding us to do push-ups or the "dry land" swim). We also had to run everywhere we went and shout the word "Airborne".

On the American base in Fort Bragg, North Carolina, I remember there were "monkey bars" in front of the mess (meal) halls. The trainees had to climb hand-over-hand along a sort of horizontal ladder, as part of the meal line up. Those who slipped and fell had to go back to the end of the line up. The bottom line was that trainees either got a stronger grip or went hungry.

Following are four basic methods[xxviii] that you can use to set up your own action environment to improve your fitness and overall health:

1. Re-arrange Your Surroundings

Re-arranging your surroundings provides several options. If you respond best to visual stimulus, you can put up motivational quotes, written reminders or pictures of athletes that inspire you. If what you need is a motivational nudge, you can move your bed near a window to catch the morning sun or put an exercise mat in the middle of your living room so that it is the first thing you see when you come home. I usually keep a gym bag full of workout gear by the front door as a reminder.

2. Find a New Location

The old saying, "a change is as good as a rest" is true for most people and just having something different to look at while you work out can be refreshing. If you've been working out at home or in the office, try a new location such as a park, gym, community center or training area. It is far easier for the majority of people to train in a place where exercise is the norm, this will likely help to boost your motivation.

3. Relocate People

Relocating people is about keeping the right company for certain situations, like physical activity. Training buddies can help keep each other motivated (or drag each other down). Try to train and talk with fitness-oriented people and avoid less motivated people. It is hard enough changing your habits without hearing snide remarks from other people. Be very selective who you share your goals with.

4. Change the Time of the Activity

Optimizing the time of day when you engage in an activity can be helpful for both physical training and weight control. Some people have higher energy levels first thing in the morning — or at midday — than they do later on. If this is you, take full advantage of timing to schedule your activities. I used to teach a Pilates fitness class during lunch hour and then eat a light lunch at my desk before carrying on with my work. I found that I got more done this way and stayed more alert during the day than I had previously when I stayed at my desk and ate a large lunch in one sitting. Speaking of eating, sometimes cooking the next day's meal right *after* you eat your evening meal can help prevent over-eating. This way, because you are already full, there is less of a tendency to nibble and sample the meal during cooking.

The key to making the environmental approach work is being aware of how different elements in your surroundings affect you. If you haven't already, make a list of all of the positive people, places, times and opportunities for exercise and eating right. Work at making these situations happen. Next, make a list of the all of the negative people, places, times and events that influence inactivity and poor health habits, then work at avoiding these situations. Above all, keep negative behaviors away from your new environments (e.g. smoking or eating junk food at a gym). Like a military operation, use every situation to your advantage.

RELAPSES

A good plan always takes into account the human tendency to slide back into old habits. Unfortunately, when it happens, many people have a tendency to beat themselves up over missing a workout or try to catch up by doing multiple workouts or starving themselves as punishment. You need to expect, and learn to accept, the occasional setback in any diet or training program. This is why it is important to plan ahead to prevent “falling off of the wagon”.

Let’s look at some typical scenarios:

Avoidable situations

If you know your weaknesses, certain places can be avoided. For example, if pastries are your downfall, rather than frequenting a coffee shop that sells pastries, you can choose to go to one that doesn’t. Or at least avoid that coffee shop during the first month of your program when your new habits are forming.

Unavoidable situations

If, due to business or other commitments, you cannot avoid a place like the coffee shop that sells pastries, you can always bring the exact change needed for your tea or coffee or choose to sit with your back to the display case.

Overreaction to occasional setbacks

There is something about human nature that strives to keep things the same. I have yet to meet even one person who has *never* had a relapse back into a bad habit. Even the most disciplined people will miss a week of workouts, eat two dozen muffins in a day or go on a week of partying. I get small relapses all of the time. It is not a big deal *unless you make it a big deal.* When you do have a setback, instead of beating yourself up emotionally, take the time to review all of the times that you stayed with the program. Then get back on the wagon and keep moving forward.

Counterproductive self-talk

Counterproductive self-talk is what I like to call a "what's the use" attitude. Here are some examples: "I'm never going to be a super athlete, so why should I bother exercising at all?" or "Everyone else is way ahead of me/better than me, so what's the point?" It is important to recognize this kind of behavior for what it is, your mind's knee jerk response to fatigue. Remind yourself that fatigue is just a temporary condition and as your body gets stronger, this little voice will eventually disappear.

Too much too soon

Trying to do too much too soon is one of the most common reasons for the failure of a new fitness program. I know two different people who have attempted to run a full marathon after just a few weeks of mild training, with no previous experience. As a youth, I recall that I was constantly trying to imitate advanced strength building routines without using the proper technique or incorporating the necessary elements of rest and nutrition into my regime. Over the years, I have seen hundreds of poorly conditioned people at various gyms push themselves beyond their fitness level for a couple of weeks and then disappear. As the saying goes, eat your elephant one bite at a time. Progress, not perfection is the goal.

Too much of a good thing

Over-training is a common problem with many fitness enthusiasts. The symptoms of over-training include: an accelerated heart rate, sleeplessness, tendency to be injury-prone, fatigue and staleness. Unfortunately, some of us get a bit of a high from over-training and find it difficult to stop exercising. If you think that you are burning out, try a couple of light days of training or change up your routines. You will often find that you come back even stronger than before. Keep in mind, that while exercise is an important part of a healthy lifestyle, you must remember to eat, rest and sleep, as well.

Planning isn't about perfect

I used to skip planning with the belief that it was taking up valuable training time. Whereas, a cyclist friend of mine, made meticulous training plans. Every workout, he knew exactly what he wanted to improve. I began to take notice when he surpassed me in skill and strength training within a short period. After that, I found that my progress was far better when I at least had some kind of plan to follow. The danger with some plans is that they can lead you into that popular all-or-nothing kind of attitude. Some perfectionists will refuse to train unless it is for a full hour in their favorite gym or only with certain equipment. Since time, equipment, food and rest are not always fit your schedule, you have to occasionally make adjustments for typical disruptions. For instance, if you've had to work late and not yet had supper, you can still eat a light supper, do some of your exercises and then eat the rest of your supper later. You cannot expect to have perfect workouts, meals, etc. every time. Some training is better than none. Think progress, not perfection.

PUTTING IT ALL TOGETHER

Ultimately, your stomach flattening workouts will give you increased strength and energy: if you apply them. Despite distractions and interruptions related to family, career, education, accidents or even the occasional natural disaster, there is always going to be some way of overcoming your obstacles.

I hope that you enjoyed Stomach Flattening. If you would like to receive more information on books, courses and information, I will put you on my VIP mailing list. We would love to hear of your success. Go to www.stomachflattening.com

Sincerely,

Doug Setter, Bsc.

www.2ndwindbodyscience.com

APPENDIX A : METABOLIC TYPE TEST (Based on *The Balance* by Oz Garcia)

---

i Yesudian, Selvarajan and Haich, Elisabeth (1953) *Yoga and Health*..................... Harper and Row Publishers: New York.

ii Borugian, M.J, Sheps, S.B, Kim-Sing, C, Olivotto, I.A., Van Patten, C, Dunn, B.P., Coldman, A.J., Potter, J.D., Gallagher, R.P. &Hislop, T.G. (2003) Am. J. Epdemiol Nov. 158:963-968. . . . . Note: High insulin levels have been associated with increased risk of breast cancer and poorer survival after a breast cancer diagnosis. **Waist-to-hip ratio** (WHR) is a marker for insulin resistance and hyperinsulinemia.

iii Staffieri Taffieri, J.R (1967). A study of social stereotype of body image in children. . . . . *Journal of Personality and Social Psychology,* 7, 101-104.

iv An abdominal crunch is performed by lying on your back and curling your upper body forward so that the shoulder blades are off of the ground.

v Yesudian, Selvarajan and Haich, Elisabeth (1953) *Yoga and Health*. . . . . Harper and Row Publishers: New York.

vi Ibid. p.117.

vii Christensen, Alice (1995) *20-Minute Yoga Workouts*. Ballantine Books: New York.

viii Schoenfeld, Brad (2000) *Sculpting Her Body Perfect.* Human Kinetics: Windsor. p.156.

ix Null, Gary, PhD (1999) *Gary Null's Ultimate Anti-Aging Program.* p. 297-298.

x Stefansson, V (1964) *Discovery: T he Autobiography of Vilhjalmur Stefansson*. . . . . McGraw-Hill : New York. 1964.

xi Kirschmann, John D. with Dunne, Lavon J. (1984) *Nutrition Almanac.* McGraw-Hill: New York.

xii Fredericks, Carlton, Ph.D. (1988) *Psycho-Nutrition.* Berkley Books: New York.

xiii Ibid.

xiv Pearson, Durk and Shaw, Sandy (1983) *Life Extension: A Practical Scientific Approach*. . . . . Warner Books, Inc.:New York. P.370.

xv Mathews-Larson (1997) *7 Weeks to Sobriety.* Ballantine Books: New York.

xvi Fredericks, Carlton, Ph.D. (1988) *Psycho-Nutrition.* Berkley Books: New York.

xvii Garcia, Oz w/Kolberg, Sharyn (1998) *The Balance*. . . . . Regan Books: New York. P.19.

xviii Ibid.

xix Banting, William (1864) *On Corpulence,* Harrison: London.

xx A friend of mine fell susceptible to a blood disease after fasting for several months. . . . . From his weakened state, a former blood disease re-emerged and he died. . . . . Fasting can have its own mild high and should be treated cautiously.

xxi Mackarness, Richard (1976) *Not All In The Mind.* Pan Books Ltd.: London.

xxii Gawain, Shakti (1978) *Creative Visualization.* Bantam Books: New York. P. 80-84.

xxiii Martin, Garry, Pear, Joseph (1999) *Behavior Modification: What it is and How to do it.* Prentice Hall P.27.

xxiv Ibid.

xxv Ibid. p.177-178.

xxvi Ibid.

xxvii Ibid.

xxviii Ibid.

1. Do you tend to get angry? a. Easily

b. Almost never
c. Occasionally

2. Do you tend to get anxious?
    a. Easily
    b. Almost never
    c. Occasionally

3. Your appetite is:
    a. Above normal
    b. Below normal
    c. Normal

4. You find it easy to:
    a. Lose weight
    b. Gain weight
    c. Maintain weight

5. Your hair is usually:
    a. Dry
    b. Oily
    c. Normal

6. Your skin is usually:
    a. Dry
    b. Oily
    c. Normal

7. Bedtime eating makes you:
    a. Toss and turn all night
    b. Feel good
    c. Indifferent

8. During the day, you:
    a. Sometimes forget to eat
    b. Get hungry often
    c. Eat only 3 times per day

9. Emotionally, you tend towards:
    a. A hot temper
    b. Calm, cool and collected
    c. Occasional emotional upsets

10. You exercise:
    a. Frequently and enjoy it
    b. Seldom, and dislike it
    c. Sometimes and enjoy it

11. You fall asleep:
    a. Easily
    b. With difficulty
    c. Within half an hour

12. You feel fatigue:
    a. Seldom
    b. Often
    c. Occasionally

13. If exercising, you like to choose:
    a. Intense aerobic exercise
    b. Weights and machines
    c. Either or

14. Your blood sugar is usually
    a. Low
    b. High
    c. Normal

15. Your breakfast is usually:
    a. Skipped
    b. Large
    c. Average

16. You like raw salad and vegetables:
    a. Quite a bit
    b. Indifferent
    c. Sometimes

17. You tend to feel too warm:
    a. Very rarely
    b. Frequently
    c. Rarely

18. You are most alert:
    a. Bright and early
    b. Around noon
    c. Whenever you get up

19. Around evening, you tend to:
    a. Go to bed early
    b. Come alive
    c. Gradually slow down

20. Regardless of what you eat, you:
    a. Have trouble gaining weight
    b. Gain weight easily
    c. Have stable weight

21. Your stamina is:
    a. Above normal
    b. Low
    c. Normal

Total the letters. A's = Fast Burners, B's = Slow Burners, C's = Mixed Burners.

APPENDIX B: WORKOUT JOURNAL

Starting weight___________

Measurements __________________________________

Month________

Sunday	**Monday**	**Tuesday**	**Wednesday**	**Thursday**	**Friday**	**Saturday**
workout, eat, rest						

Total number of workouts ___/30 days

DIET: B = Bad, OK= Okay G = Good.

APPENDIX C: BEHAVIOR-CHANGING CONTRACT

LIFESTYLE CONTRACT
Designed by Doug Setter

1. My specific goals for life-style change are:

____

2. Short-term self-control goals are:

____

3. I will journal my progress every __________ and review in ______days on the date of: __________________.

4. To minimize the causes of the problem, I will:

____

5. Rewards for short-term goals:

____

6. Minor punishments for straying from program:
(eg. No music for a day)

____

7. Additional steps for success:

____

________________	________________	________________________
(Date)	(Your Signature)	(Supporter's Signature)

REFERENCES

68401688R00065

Made in the USA
Lexington, KY
09 October 2017